Additional Prais

Grieving the Death of a Pet

"*Grieving the Death of a Pet* is a must-read for everyone facing the intense pain that comes with losing a cherished animal companion. Betty J. Carmack's deep understanding of the grieving process and her profound respect for the human-animal bond shine through on every page. With real stories of people and their beloved pets, she offers coping strategies, comfort, insight, and inspiration. *Grieving the Death of a Pet* delivers hope and help. It is a handbook for healing and a moving tribute to the powerful connection we have with our pets."

—Ed Sayres, President, San Francisco Society for the Prevention of Cruelty to Animals

"This is a book that will touch your heart and help it to heal. I was crying before I finished the introduction. We all must learn to deal with loss if we are to survive. As a physician, I know how destructive it can be to deny the loss and bury it within one's self. The death of a beloved pet puts us in touch with all our losses. Betty J. Carmack's words of wisdom, coming from her experience with the pain of loss, can help you to heal your life and wounds. The wise know our bodies are impermanent and the only thing of permanence is love. Read on and help make yourself and your beloved immortal."

—Bernie Siegel, MD, author of *Love, Medicine & Miracles* and *Prescriptions for Living*

"Those who can say 'it's just a pet' won't need this book. For those who know better, Betty J. Carmack teaches how to fully honor the loss of a truly beloved companion. The lessons of grief for our animals have much to teach us about how to grieve for the human companions in our lives. They are lessons well learned."

—Megory Anderson, MA, founding director of the Sacred Dying Foundation, author of *Sacred Dying: Creating Rituals for Embracing the End of Life*

⁓

"Betty J. Carmack offers readers a gift through her narratives and kind guidance for experiencing the loss of a pet. This is a book about connection, relationships, and love that make up the rich landscape of the caring lives of pet guardians. *Grieving the Death of a Pet* makes a clear point: Pet loss is *not* the minor league of grief."

—Harold Ivan Smith, D.Min., grief counselor, author of *Grieving the Death of a Mother, On Grieving the Death of a Father,* and *When Your Friend Dies.*

⁓

"*Grieving the Death of a Pet* offers the nurturing supportive hug that we all need when we experience the loss of a kindred spirit. Betty J. Carmack gently nurses you through this challenging process. Read it, weep, and heal!"

—Allen M. Schoen, MS, DVM, professor, and author, *Kindred Spirits: How the Remarkable Bond between Humans and Animals Can Change the Way We Live*

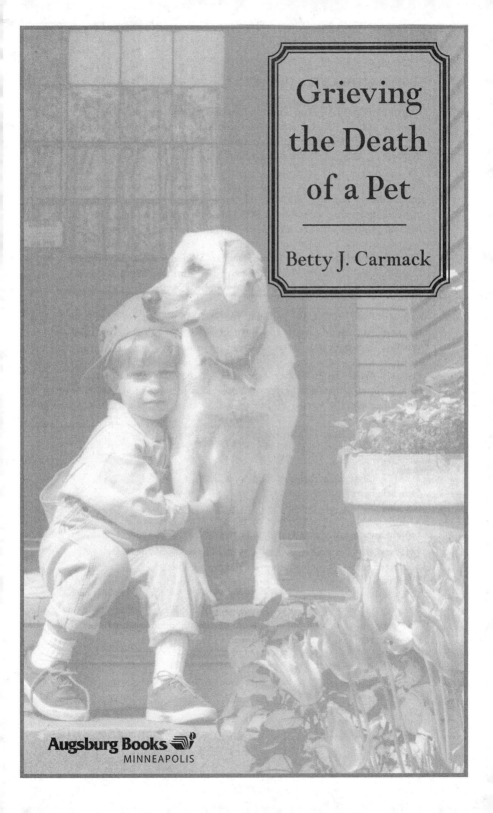

Grieving
the Death
of a Pet

Betty J. Carmack

Augsburg Books
MINNEAPOLIS

GRIEVING THE DEATH OF A PET

Large-quantity purchases or custom editions of this book are available at a dis-
count from the publisher. For more information, contact the sales department
at Augsburg Fortress, Publishers, 1-800-328-4648, or write to: Sales Director,
Augsburg Fortress, Publishers, P.O. Box 1209, Minneapolis, MN 55440-1209.

Scripture passages are from the Revised Standard Version of the Bible, copyright
© 1946, 1952, 1971, 1989 by the Division of Christian Education of the
National Council of the Churches of Christ in the USA. Used by permission.

Page 107: From Jack Pantaleo's musical, *The Gospel According to The Angel Julius*
the song, "You Are My Beloved." Copyright © 1993 and 1999 (revised) Jack
Pantaleo, Playwright and Composer. Used with permission.

Page 118: From Oprah Winfrey, September 23, 2001, Yankee Stadium, New
York [This was a memorial/prayer service for the September 11 victims, fami-
lies, and nation.]

Book and cover design by Michelle L. N. Cook
Cover art from Getty Images

Library of Congress Cataloging-in-Publication Data
Carmack, Betty J., 1941-
Grieving the death of a pet / Betty J. Carmack.
p. cm.
ISBN 0-8066-4348-X (pbk.: alk. paper)
1. Pet owners—Psychology. 2. Pets—Death—Psychological aspects.
3. Bereavement—Psychological aspects. 4. Grief. I. Title.
SF411.47 .C374 2003
155.9'37—dc21   2002013177

Manufactured in the U.S.A.

08   7   8   9   10

To our animal companions—past, present, and future—who grace and bless our lives

CONTENTS

Acknowledgments

With deepest gratitude I thank:

My parents, Willa Mima Nooe Carmack and Iris Walter Carmack, for your lifelong belief in me and your abiding wisdom—the value of working hard, doing one's best, and living one's dreams—you are my heroes.

My sisters, Sally Carmack Anderson and Nancy Carmack Greene, for your loving encouragement and behind-the-scenes photo shoot.

Carol-Ann D'Amico, for your never-ending patience and love—without your support, both endearing and enduring, this writing endeavor would have been entirely different.

Jack Pantaleo, for your unceasing faith in my ability to write this book and your continual wise counsel and expert assistance so graciously given.

Susan Chernak McElroy, kindred spirit, for your eloquent and thoughtful foreword and your ongoing life's work that nurtures the holy partnerships we have with our animals.

Dr. Harold Ivan Smith, for your instrumental role in introducing me to Augsburg Fortress, Publishers, and for your many important contributions to our knowledge of grief and loss.

Dr. John Lantz, for helping me have the time to write.

Françoise Etchenique, behind-the-scenes extraordinaire—you saved me more times than I could ever count. You are my miracle worker.

Sally Anderson, Willa Mima Nooe Carmack, Iris Walter Carmack, Carol-Ann D'Amico, Nancy Greene, Betty Greene Grogan, Elaine Mannon, and Jack Pantaleo, for your careful reviews of the manuscript drafts and your immensely valuable critiques.

Martha Rosenquist, Michael Wilt, and Michelle L. N. Cook, editors, and Marilee Reu, publicist, at Augsburg Fortress, Publishers, for your continual and expert help, careful attention to detail, and timely responses to my many questions.

Augsburg Fortress, Publishers, for giving me the opportunity to write about a topic close to my heart, and for your readiness to see its importance.

My extraordinary family, friends, and colleagues who faithfully asked, "How's the book?" You cheered me on throughout this whole pursuit as you offered and gave me your help, honest feedback, and support.

The hundreds of pet parents who have shared your stories of your relationships with and your grief for your loved animal companions—how often I felt I was on sacred ground as I listened to your voices.

Author's Note

This book marks the twentieth anniversary of my work as a nurse in pet loss counseling. Throughout the years I've had the privilege of walking the path with more than two thousand people who are anticipating or experiencing grief for the loss of their pets. I have always tried to earn and keep the sacred trust of those who have confided in me. To write this book about the experience of grief for beloved companion animals would be impossible without the stories of many people. The stories in this book are real; they have not been fictionalized. I'm indebted to the countless people who have shared their stories of grief. They've trusted me with their stories, the feelings that accompanied those stories, and the meaning and significance of their grief, and I've honored that trust. Most of the people I interviewed gave me permission to use their real names and their animals' real names. For those who preferred a pseudonym for themselves and their animal companions, this preference has been honored. Where pseudonyms are used, the essence of the person's story remains unchanged.

FOREWORD

I lost my "forever dog," Keesha, in 1983 on the first day of my annual vacation. She was only ten and a half years old, yet riddled head to tail with advanced melanoma—tumors sprouting daily like twisted mushrooms on her delicate head and lean flanks. Somehow, I got through the afternoon of her euthanasia. Somehow, I helped place her in a storage refrigerator because the humane society crematorium was temporarily on the blink. Somehow, I drove home without injuring myself or other drivers. But when I got home and saw the huge bone I had brought for her last night's "chew fest" sitting lonely and untouched on the living room floor, I lost it.

From the marrow of my bones, the sobs came and would not stop. I think I cried nonstop for most of the next two weeks and returned to work with eyes as red as stoplights. Years before her death, I would say to anyone who would listen that on the day Keesha died, my life would never be the same. It was true. I sit here at my desk these many years after her passing, looking at a charcoal portrait of her that hangs over my computer. After all this time, I still feel the tug of her soft eyes on my heart. New and beloved dogs have come to fill that heart, yet there remains the velvet-lined, eternally empty corner that houses the memory of who and what we were together.

I believe that the loss of a beloved animal companion is like no other loss because our relationships with animals are like no other. Our culture tells us that an animal companion is an engaging toy, and that our grief over its death is alarming and ill-placed. And our culture is just flat wrong. As a survivor of advanced cancer myself, I believe that the love and comfort of animals in great measure graced me with recovery. This being the case, I would not be one to take kindly to any cultural diminishment of our relationship with "the other." Bluntly put, "Them's fightin' words" in my world. Animals are more to us than we know. Their partnership with us is a holy one that endures across a lifetime and possibly beyond.

For most of us, the loss of an animal will be our first experience with death. In this way, animals give us a most precious and intimate gift—the opportunity to learn how to live through grief, and to learn that we *can* live through grief. Stepping into this blazing cauldron of loss and pain, we emerge hardened not into stone, but into diamonds, aware now that we can face almost anything and survive. If we diminish the loss in our own eyes, subdue it, tell ourselves it has no meaning, then we will deflate the enormous value of this gift. A sixteen-year-old girl wrote to me upon the death of her mare and foal, lost in a tragic barn fire, "I leaned on my friends, I leaned on my family. I cried and cried and cried, and when I stopped crying, I realized I could survive anything." Who else but animals could have delivered such a powerful message to such a young woman in a way that would not cripple but empower her? I often find it is animals who are the messengers of this kind of harsh but necessary wisdom.

After writing and lecturing for almost seven years now about what animals bring to our experience of life, health, and grieving, I have come to understand that the reason it is so difficult for us to express the depth of the animal-human bond—and thus better explain its potential for health of body, mind, and spirit—is because our language truly lacks the words. Eskimos have many words for snow. We have only one for "dog," and therein lies much of the problem. It is hard for us to fully accept this bond between us and the others when we don't have words to explain its fuller meaning. I believe this is why science has a near-impossible time getting its research-loving hands around the "pet lover thing." Not only does the animal-human bond defy statistics and numbers and double-blind studies, but it defies words as well.

Yet there is another, perhaps even better way to know something truly and deeply than through words that define and categorize. It is a more roundabout way requiring imagination, heart, and openness. It is a way that uses words, as a pathway rather than as a destination point. It is the way of story. The tellers of myths and fables knew this—that ideas and experiences that cannot be penetrated by definition can be illuminated by a well-told story.

This, then, is the value of Betty Carmack's work. In exploring the deeper meaning of pet loss, she has moved into territory that is beyond language, and has instinctively chosen the wise path of story. Stories bypass the intellect, which has nothing to offer us in the dark forest of grief anyway, and guide us on a direct, healing path to the heart and the emotions. How comforting, almost expected, it is to encounter animals in this land. For all time, it has been their way to speak to us—never through our heads, but through the other modes of our experience and expression. We communicate with our animal companions through our touch, our gut instincts, our emotions, our spirits. Here is the land beyond words where animals do their best work, guiding us along dark paths through a world of pain, confusion, and loss. It is a journey that will hold us in good stead, granting us a lens through which to explore every other loss in our life—those past and those yet to come.

In the stories contained here, you will find a world of "other" wisdom on the finer points of letting go with grace, maturity, blessing, and, eventually, perhaps a kind of quiet joy. You will see that the phrase, "It was just an animal" is the observance of a fool—a sad fool with a hard heart and very few good stories in his or her own grief-management repair kit. And you will come to know the animals whose deaths, as told in these pages may become a profound teaching for you.

Settle down gently and let these finely told stories scurry past your head and take up lodging in the inner chambers of your heart, where all true learning and healing must come home to rest.

—Susan Chernak McElroy, author of *Animals as Teachers and Healers: True Stories and Reflections* and *Heart in the Wild: A Journey of Discovery with the Animals of the Wilderness*

OVERVIEW

"I never cried this much when my family member died," and "I knew it was going to hurt, but I didn't think it would be this bad" are two frequently expressed sentiments of grief for a loved animal companion. In the twenty years that I've worked with grieving pet parents, I've listened to stories and seen, heard, and felt profound grief. I've been a witness to the journey of grief for a beloved companion animal, and I've experienced my own grief. I've learned that healing can come.

This book is a witness to the lived experience of grief for the loss of a companion animal. When I use the term "lived experience," I mean living with and through an experience with all the feelings, thoughts, and behaviors that accompany that event. The importance, depth, and extent of pet loss grief is described and reflected through personal stories and vignettes of pet loss experiences. I tell my stories of my own pet losses and weave them through the book as a way to both personalize the book and engage you, the reader.

The scripture passage from Ecclesiastes 3:1-8 serves as a unifying theme and grounds the book:

"For everything there is a season, and a time for every matter under heaven:

a time to be born, and a time to die;

a time to plant, and a time to pluck up what is planted;

a time to kill, and a time to heal;

a time to break down, and a time to build up;

a time to weep, and a time to laugh;

a time to mourn, and a time to dance;

a time to cast away stones, and a time to gather stones together;

a time to embrace, and a time to refrain from embracing;
a time to seek, and a time to lose;
a time to keep, and a time to cast away;
a time to rend, and a time to sew;
a time to keep silence, and a time to speak;
a time to love, and a time to hate;
a time for war, and a time for peace."

I've selected this passage for several reasons.

First, it's one of my favorites, and it feels natural in a book about living through the experience of pet loss. One of the themes in this book is that of chronological time and its relationship to the experience of loss. In interviews, one-on-one sessions, and support groups, people have consistently discussed their grief in terms of time. There's a temporal quality to their descriptions. Time has been a marker. Time has been contextual. In conversation after conversation, I've heard references to the time before the animal's death, the time surrounding the actual death, and the time after the death. Specific references to events are delineated and depicted in temporal terms.

Second, this scripture is universal in its relationship and relevance to people of all spiritual faiths and practices. The passage links spirituality to life's rhythms and events, to life's ebb and flow, and to grief and healing regardless of one's particular spiritual beliefs. Spirituality not only gives consciousness and meaning to our grief but also heals our grief. This passage helps to offer hope for healing and the belief that something positive can come from something sad and tragic. Because it transcends denominations and religions, I believe it helps interweave the experiential and the spiritual.

Several other themes are found throughout the book. The overriding theme is the lived experience of grief for a beloved companion animal, captured in the voices of those who grieve. I believe we can learn from others' experience. This book legitimizes the experience of grieving pet parents who look to have their feelings validated. It is my hope that when they read this book, they will see they are not alone in their feelings. Nor are they "crazy" for feeling their emotions or having their experiences.

This book is a tribute to the strength of the human-companion animal bond and the relationships people have with their pets. I use people's voices to reflect the depth of this bond. In fact, it's because of that depth of love between people and their companion animals that this book is needed.

The dimension of spirituality is also incorporated into the book. This is reflected not only in vignettes and quotations, but also in poetry and prayers. Spirituality includes an appreciation for the diversity of spiritual beliefs and practices. While grief includes tears, sorrow, and hurt, it can also mean coming closer to Spirit and God.

Another theme is that of hope. I offer the hope that, with time, healing can occur. The passage from Ecclesiastes holds out a spiritual basis of hope and reassurance. My own story, and those of others, reinforces the healing that can come from grief.

The experiences of pet loss captured in this book are not reflective of everyone. I know that. Some people who lose an animal have no connection to what is written here because their experiences are completely different. But what is described in this book does reflect the experiences of the hundreds of people with whom I've had the privilege of working. This book puts a face on their lived experience of pet loss and gives them a voice. It tells them clearly their grief does matter.

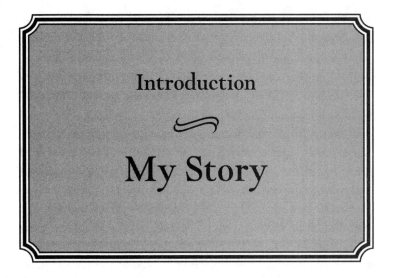

Introduction

∽

My Story

"How was your vacation?" people would ask, expecting a positive answer. My answer was tears, feelings of nausea, a racing heart, a knotted stomach, and trembling. Somehow I got the story out. I wanted to talk about it, and I didn't want to talk about it. I simply didn't have the words to describe what had happened. I could tell the objective story but not the subjective story. I simply didn't have the words in July 1978.

Now I finally have the words. I can now tell my story. I still consider it one of the worst days of my life.

It started off as a lazy rafting trip down the Trinity River on the last day of my vacation. The Trinity, gentle and slow, carried us down the river: Rocky, my ten-year-old dachshund; my friend, Bill; and me. Rocky was resting peacefully in the raft, even sleeping at times, while we floated along. We had almost reached the place we would take our raft out, deflate it, and head for home, taking with us a lovely memory in a rejuvenating week in the mountains.

In the next minute my life changed forever; there could be no going back. The river currents had pulled our raft into low-hanging branches along the river's edge. When I saw the branches knock Bill out of the raft into the river, I made the split-second decision that we should all stay together. I grabbed Rocky by the collar and pulled him overboard with me. I've thought about the wisdom of that decision countless times and wondered what the outcome would have been if I had stayed in the raft with Rocky. The speed with which I made my decision was based, no doubt, on my feeling of inadequacy of managing the raft alone. I had no way of knowing the outcome of that decision. The next few minutes are confusing as to particulars, but the emotion of the moment is forever embedded in me. I'm not a swimmer, and I was struggling, with Bill's help, to keep afloat while holding on to Rocky with my right hand. At some point in that struggle, I simply could not physically hold on to Rocky and continue to hold on to branches or try to swim or whatever I was attempting to do. I don't remember all the details, but I do remember the moment of letting go of his collar and seeing him float down the river with his little head above the water. That is my last image of him. I never saw him again, and I never learned what happened to him, but I think that most likely he drowned.

I suppose he could have made it to the river's edge and gotten out. If that had happened, I suppose he could have survived somehow or been adopted, or whatever—but I doubt all that. I ran an ad in the local newspaper with a reward, but I never heard a word. On some level, I need to believe he drowned so I have some explanation . . . but I can't be sure.

The ride back to San Francisco was unreal. I could not believe that Rocky wasn't with me. He had been with me for ten years, and in a minute he was gone. The disbelief and profound emptiness were overwhelming. He used to ride on the floor of the passenger's side beside my feet. I loved that I could look down, see him, and feel his little body next to me. I had always felt complete when he was close by; now I felt utterly torn apart from him, violently so.

My life changed irrevocably. Rocky's loss taught me how deeply we grieve for our loved animals, the intensity of pain, the length of time it can last, and how one's life can be forever changed. I would have given anything for a pet-loss support group, a place I could go and talk about the heartache, sorrow, guilt, and grief I was feeling. I learned firsthand that grief for a companion animal matters, even though we live in a world that reminds us repeatedly that grief for an animal doesn't count as much as grief for a person. The anniversary of his death taught me the reality of anniversary grief.

Just as I have the words and can now tell my story, I can also tell the stories of many other individuals who have lived the grief that comes from losing a loved companion animal. They have shared their stories with me. Now I can also give voice to their words. Throughout this book I will tell additional parts of my story about Rocky—and Puccini—and Sunshine—and Sarah. I will tell the story of my grief and my healing so you can know with certainty that I, too, have been on this path. I don't write only as a nurse and grief counselor. I also write as someone who has lived with the grief and has been able to heal and transform deep sorrow into something positive. My words and story may give hope to those who don't yet believe they can ever feel better or come to a place of healing.

Chapter I

A Time to Love

"a time to love" (Eccles. 3:8)

Don't tell me he was "just a dog," he was my best friend, my family, my baby. Don't ask me if I've "gotten over it yet"; I'll never get over it.
—*Participant, pet loss support group*

With great love comes great grief. If the love weren't so strong, the intense grief and sorrow at the time of an animal companion's death wouldn't be so wrenching. Grieving pet parents look back on their relationships with their animals and long for their presence again. They search for words to describe what was so remarkable about their pets and what they miss so intensely now. It comes down to the animals' central importance in their lives and the ways in which their lives were greatly enriched. Their inter-connected-ness with and emotional investment in their beloved companion animals are evident in the many evocative stories they tell. They describe pure, complete, and unconditional love.

This chapter consists of a synthesis of people's voices and their stories. Their grief is a witness and tribute to the depth of connectedness to their animal companions. There's a conscious appreciation and mindfulness of their animals' characteristics, qualities, and place in their lives. What was it about these companion animals that made them so integral to people's lives?

ALWAYS THERE FOR ME

Many voices spoke of the loss of abiding presence—the constancy and stability that animal companions bring to our lives. Their pets were there for them when they went through difficult times and events. Through all of the ups and downs—ending relationships, divorces, life-threatening illnesses and accidents, deaths, job transitions, moves to new homes, painful memories of past abuse—their animals had been their one stable and constant presence. To lose this reassuring equilibrium and balance is to be painfully shaken at the core of one's being.

There is an unmistakable interdependence between us and our companion animals. Not only do they depend on us, but we depend on them. Betty acknowledged this awareness:

> Katie [her dog] has been the one constant in my life. She's been around longer than any man I've been with or any job I've had. She's been through so much with me. I really don't think I would be here without her. She kept me sane when I was at my lowest. I knew I couldn't leave her. I didn't want to leave her.

Robert reinforced this insight when he said:

> Basko had an intuitive understanding of what I was going through, what I was feeling, and what I needed. I could talk to him, and on some level he grasped what I was trying to say. Non-human animals are often much more intuitive than we are.

The experience of an animal's steadfastness is prevalent. Patricia spoke of her dog, Auggie:

My mid-thirties and mid-forties were pretty volatile years. Auggie was pretty much the only constant and mainstay through all the changes and instability of relationships, jobs, and moves. When I realized he wasn't going to be there, it was like, oh my God, I won't be able to get through this.

Debra supported this idea when she described her dog:

Addison was my companion. I have good friends, but I lived with Addison and went through some of the roughest times in my life, and he was here for me. He helped guide me through a decade of my life.

A similar experience came through in Carol-Ann's story. She told me about the presence of Lizzie-Beth, her dog, during a six week recovery from an ankle injury: "She was my little therapist lying beside me every day. She wasn't an official therapy dog, but she became *my* therapy dog."

People continually confirm that their animals ground them through some of their most wrenching experiences. A grieving young woman spoke of her dog's unwavering presence during one of her darkest moments:

A few years ago when I had experienced a breakthrough in my therapy and recalled one of the most painful episodes in my life, I had broken down, sobbing on the floor in the kitchen. When I had the flashback, I also got sick. I was lying on the floor by myself, and he came in and sat down right next to me and just stayed with me. He had been sleeping in the living room. I can't believe he knew to come and just be with me. I was a mess, and he came and just sat with me. I was grateful for that.

Animal companions are described as our anchors. Mary Lou's Al-Anon sponsor died. Her sister had a serious relapse, resulting in considerable family disruption; her daughter, son, and husband each lost their jobs. As a result, her son became homeless and lived out of his car. She experienced an extremely difficult interpersonal relationship as a volunteer on an international mission. And, Rascal, her dog, died. Unequivocally, she said that losing Rascal was the loss that most distressed her, because he had been her anchor through all her other losses and stress.

Likewise, Nancy captured her recognition of the stabilizing force of animal companions when she said:

> Who can say that our pets aren't actually angels placed into our lives by God to look after us in this earthly life? For who has not survived trouble and hard times because of the total love and commitment of a pet? And who does not remember a pet's love and miss that more than the people who may have turned their backs on us?

Animal companions can be the predominant motivation for people to turn their lives around. Pali told of being homeless and around drugs since childhood. She described the chaotic time of living on the street enmeshed in the drug culture and the twenty-four-hour companionship of her dog, Leadbelly. She credits him with being the one who helped her turn her life around. She began her treatment program to become clean and sober *for him* to get *him* off the streets. She wouldn't have made that move *for herself* alone, but she could and did *for him*. Pali kept repeating what a "huge thing" it was that Leadbelly had done for her.

Similarly, Steve also conveyed how the love of his parrot provided him with both physical and emotional health benefits:

> I got her at a pretty difficult time. I was in recovery, and I felt pretty unlovable. She changed that, and that was a gift. I thought if a little bird likes you, you can't be that bad. I was

very taken aback by the healing I felt every day after feeding her. I'd go there feeling very stressed but after cuddling with her and feeding her, I was much more peaceful.

Companion animals provide their steady presence through multiple losses and deaths. Sharron described how her dog, Gigi, saved her sanity after her own illness, her sister's death, and her partner's death: "She was a godsend, both during my cancer and during losing Stan. I mourned Stan very deeply. I became reclusive. Gigi made my being reclusive okay."

Steve also acknowledged his bird's grounding presence during his numerous losses of friends:

One time when my best friend died, I said to Porkchop, "You're sleeping with me in the bed." So I got a towel and put it right next to me and put pillows around it, and she just sat there and slept with me all night.

We've heard stories of animals' ongoing devotion and unceasing fidelity even after their owners' death—dogs that still go to the train station daily to wait for the train, as well as animals that continue to sit or lie beside a person's body. In many instances these faithful animals have to be physically removed. Boots, a devoted Boston Terrier, was found sitting on the chest of his master who had died in bed several days earlier. Neighbors, concerned when they hadn't seen the man or Boots, called the police, who found them together.

To lose such enduring devotion and loyalty is exceedingly painful.

RECIPROCAL NURTURANCE

Additionally, there's the loss of reciprocal caring. Animal companions help us feel special, lovable, worthwhile, and unconditionally loved. I'm frequently reminded of the Prayer of St. Francis, "... *it is in giving that we receive* ..." Again and again, I hear stories from those who have felt nurtured themselves when they nurtured their animals. The ongoing care provided to animals influences the well-being and personal recovery of pet parents. Carol-Ann noted this reciprocal caring in her description:

> I am greeted by a little ray of sunshine every time I return home. My little dog, Lizzie-Beth, lifts my spirits. She's my playmate and confidante. There's an honesty about her, a living being to nurture and care for.

This two-way sensitivity and attunement to care for each other comes through in story after story. Debra described her experience of mutuality with Addison in terms of being "equals." At times he'd take care of her, and at other times, she'd take care of him.

Likewise, Patricia reinforced this dimension of reciprocity with her springer spaniel:

> At a time in my life when I didn't feel there was a lot to look forward to, I always knew I had Auggie to take care of. I don't have that anymore, and that makes me sad. My husband doesn't need me to take care of him. He's very self-sufficient. But with Auggie, if I was depressed and on the couch, he'd come over and nudge me with his nose, like, "Let's go for a walk." I'd look at him and say, "I don't feel like going for a walk. I'm sad and depressed, and I just want to lie here." He'd nudge me again and, of course, I'd get up and take him for a walk. Invariably I'd feel better being out in the sunshine, walking and breathing fresh air because my dog made me take a walk.

Following Auggie's death, Patricia lost her motivation for walks. Instead, she stayed on the couch feeling sad and depressed, knowing no one needed her to do anything. She had lost that sense of interdependence.

When we bring these animal companions into our lives, we make a promise to care for them and love them. Individuals take seriously the responsibility of caring for their animals, wanting to do right by them. Their overriding sense of trustworthiness keeps them ever mindful of their animals' safety and well-being. The idea of covenant comes to my mind. Steve summed it up this way:

> My life isn't just about me. I made the commitment to her and felt a responsibility to give her a good life. I had to come home to let her out of the cage. I had to clean her cage every day, feed her, buy her toys, and spend time with her. Birds need you and want attention. I wanted to make sure she felt loved. That bond is what I miss most, because it was just her and me.

Continuous and reciprocal unconditional love, nurturing, and mutuality—to lose this is agony.

FAMILY MEMBER, BEST FRIEND, SOUL MATE

Animal companions are highly valued family members, usually thought of and cared for as "babies" and "children." Time after time I hear, "My animals are my children; they're my family." Betty and Pat say about their cocker spaniels, Katie and Thumper, "They're like our children; we call them 'the kids.'" Recently, I was in a card shop and on the check-out counter beside me was a basket of medals. Fingering through these, I found one attached to a tag with an image of a dog and the words "My Child." The numerous tributes and memorials at Internet pet loss sites reflect a particular term of endearment, "fur babies." For my last birthday, a friend gave me a photo album entitled *My Furry Child.*

On the other hand, some people experience their animals more in the role of parent because of the protective nurturing animals provide. Dogs guard us and alert us to dangers. Some animals go from room to room, refusing to sleep at night until each family member is accounted for and in the expected place. We feel more secure because of their benevolent presence.

We buy our animal companions gifts, celebrate their birthdays, take them along on vacations—actually, we plan vacations around them. We share our meals with them and invite them onto our beds. Some nuzzle and burrow under our covers with us. They have their own lines of clothing, footwear, toys, holiday accessories, fragrances, jewelry, bedding, foods, treats, and housing—some of which are quite expensive and elaborate. We patronize ice cream stores that give them their own special cones or sundaes. Some animal companions have even served as ring bearers in weddings. "For us, they're people," says Kerry. "They're our family. They're perfect for us. We can fawn over them, fuss over them and enjoy them."

Robert told me that he and his wife Bonnie had always regarded Basko, their German shepherd, as one of their sons. Their children were grown, and they had a different kind of relationship with Basko, being dependent on him in ways they never were with their children. A considerable part of pet owners' identity is that of pet parent—pet mom, pet dad. Subsequently, when our animal companions pass on, this former identity is profoundly altered.

Words denoting relationships other than family are also frequently used: "best friend," "life partner," "soul mate," "my buddy," "love of my life," and "significant other." To experience a companion animal as a best friend or soul mate is to share a relationship at a profound level where the essence of the animal and person meet.

Steve reflected the experience of significant other when he spoke of Porkchop, his African gray parrot: "If I lay down in the afternoon and took a nap, she'd take a nap, too. We felt very much a couple."

Robert said of his close relationship to his German shepherd:

> I loved Basko more than I've ever loved another creature. He was supportive of me. I felt obligated to him. I would always try to put him first before myself, regardless of how tired I was or anything else. I was closer to him than I've ever been to another creature.

Jyl experienced her cat Muffy as her soulmate with whom she was deeply intertwined:

> We were together ten years. She was an incredible source of solace, an extraordinary being, my soulmate with a big presence. Her spiritual presence filled my home. I didn't just love her, I was in love with her. Our essences were bonded.

Some persons acknowledge experiencing a deep spiritual connection to their animal, both before and after the death. Jyl continued:

> I felt like Muffy was a high being who had come back in the body of a cat. She was like this goddess who had been sent to me, a guru, an enlightened being who was in her last incarnation when I got her. There was a magnetic field between us, where she was exquisitely attuned to me. I'll maintain forever that she wasn't just a cat.

Erica said of her cat: "Mao was an old soul. He'd probably been through a few lifetimes, and he was a wise, old, bold, little soul—such a great cat. We understood each other perfectly." Likewise, Kerry spoke of her cat's intellect: "She was so knowing that you never thought you were with a cat. That all-knowing presence was hard to give up."

A loss of such a core part of one's life is significant and devastating and can feel like part of one's body has been cut out. No one gets over that depth of loss easily.

We experience different relationships with various people in our lives. Our relationships with our friends aren't necessarily the same as those with our siblings. We have still another type of relationship with our partners and spouses. It doesn't make the relationships any less or any more. They are simply unalike.

Similarly, when we consider our animal companions, we see that we love each one differently, and no other relationships can give us what they provide. People often readily acknowledge they love their animals more than they love their siblings, parents, or partners. For others, it's not that they love their animals more, but that they have qualitatively different relationships with their animals.

SUCH A JOY

However it's discussed and whatever words are used, animal companions bring pure joy into people's lives. These beloved animals are experienced as blessings and gifts from the universe. They are described as fun and playful with joyful personalities that delight in themselves and their interactions with others.

The joy that Mao brought to Erica became part of the fabric of her everyday life:

> I had no idea it was going to be such a wondrous experience. Mao was a very special cat. I had no idea there was so much unconditional love and affection in the universe. Every single day he brought me unbelievable joy, and I told him that. Every day I took time to tell him how much I loved him and how glad I was he came to live with me.

Sharron said the hardest part of losing Gigi, her dog, was the loss of "the great joy." Each morning Sharron marveled that no matter how badly she felt after her partner, Stan, died, she had to smile because when she'd wake up, Gigi was giving her the clear message, "Okay, let's go." That quality of joy in Sharron's life was now absent.

People regularly and frequently describe the "fun piece"—the excitement, comic relief, playfulness, happiness, and bliss of their animals' everyday presence. Betty said of her dogs, "They are always doing something funny to make us laugh."

The pleasure and comfort of her animals' pure companionship was described by Pali. There were days when she didn't feel she could be around people but preferred, instead, to spend the day with her five dogs, in bed, watching movies or sleeping. "You just want to be alone with your animals. You don't have to explain to them or make up words to match how you feel." Sometimes she was physically unable to get out of bed because the blankets were so tightly wrapped from her dogs' weight. As if in a nest, comforted and warm, she'd fall back to sleep.

As I write, I seek out Sarah, my dog, to have her close. If she's on the sofa, I take my work to the sofa. If she's back under the covers, I, too, get back under the covers to write. Her physical presence is comforting and reassuring and supplies a deep-felt need only she can fill. To touch her is profoundly fulfilling. Even to look across the room or bed and see her lying there, sleeping peacefully, touches an innermost place, and I prayerfully thank her for being in my life.

This loss of pure companionship, joy, and contentment is characterized as wrenching.

DAILY INTERACTIONS AND RITUALS SHARED

Grieving pet parents describe feeling an immense void and a huge hole, "I just miss her, and I want her back." Animal companions share our regular routines. Because they live with us, they are part of numerous daily interactions, from the moment of waking until the moment of falling asleep. We wake with them on our pillows, and we go to sleep with them curled up next to us. They're with us for our morning coffee, afternoon tea, and bedtime snacks. They are present for some of our most private moments. They watch us get dressed and undressed. Not only do they bid us farewell when we leave, they also greet us when we return. They "talk" to us and let us know if we've been away too long. They are a huge presence in our lives, because we share countless moments together.

Nancy explained why, after twenty years, things still remind her of her former companions: "I guess it's because in such small ways they become such an important part of our lives. So it's the small and ordinary things that happen daily, which cause the memories to come rushing back."

Over the years I've come to know with absolute certainty that it doesn't matter what the species is. In addition to dogs and cats, I've known people who were grieving a bird, rabbit, fish, tortoise, turtle, snake, guinea pig, rat, hamster, or horse. The depth of connection, relationship, and love is what matters—not the species. It's the big and little moments we come to depend on and cherish. It's all those treasured times we miss most when they are gone.

Debra spoke of her interactions with her dog:

> We were always together. Whenever I was moving around the apartment, Addison was right with me, even in the bathroom. He slept so close to me that sometimes we'd be pushing each other to try to get space. I wanted to come home and spend my time with him.

Steve detailed how Porkchop participated in his daily routine:

> In the morning I'd get dressed and put on my clothes, and she'd say, "Bye, Pork." I always said, "Bye, Pork" when I left, so when she saw me getting dressed, she'd say, "Bye, Pork." In the evening it was just us. We would cuddle up and watch TV. I'd sit there, and she'd sit on my shoulder. She'd preen my beard, and I'd rub her head while we watched TV. If they laughed on TV, she'd laugh. She knew nighttime was her time.

He recalled the times they'd go to the park and she'd play in the grass. Often Steve would lay on the grass and sleep with Porkchop on his stomach or chest.

Our animal companions are unequivocally part of the landscape of our lives. Patricia said it was Auggie's world, and she lived in it. Robert described how his and Bonnie's life revolved around Basko. Hundreds of photos show Basko right in the middle of their activities. When they scattered the ashes of Robert's mother into the ocean, Basko was standing alongside Robert. Vacations and camping—they wouldn't go places unless they could take him with them.

The recognition that an animal companion is a gift to a person's life helps capture the essence of these relationships. That so many experience companion animals as a blessing from the universe is witness to the depth of our connections. People say it is through their animals that they learn the true meaning of the words "gift," "blessing," and "unconditional love."

"She was such a good dog and loving companion," said Sharron. "It was divine justice that I was meant to take Gigi home and care for her. She was a gift. The thing I keep repeating to myself when I'm at a loss is—I had a gift."

. . . a time to love . . .

Chapter 2

A Time to Get Ready

"a time to lose" (Eccles. 3:6)

*I felt like this big machinery, all the wheels, gears, cogs
and levers had been put into motion. They were going to
play themselves out, and I just had to go through it. I
wasn't going to have a whole lot of control over what
happened. I just had to steer Mao through the experience
as best as I could.*
　　—Erica

This chapter explores the considerable difficulties in deciding
about the care one chooses to give—or not to give—an old,
injured, or ill animal. Those whose voices speak of "getting ready"
and "saying good-bye" characterize this time as unique within the
experience of pet loss, a time like no other. Their touching stories
reflect the poignancy and emotions of this time.

"A time to lose" refers to a time of living with the unknown
and uncertainty. Life's stability, constancy, and predictability are

threatened. In the face of declining health, it's a time of persistent anticipatory losses.

> "I know the changes are coming, but please not so fast. Not yet. Not today."
>
> "We don't know how long before we'll have to make the decision."
>
> "If I get another six months with him, I'll be lucky."
>
> "How much longer will the medications work?"
>
> "When do the vet and I have 'that talk'?"
>
> "Will she get really sick one day and will that be the beginning of the end?"
>
> "One day I think I'm putting the cart before the horse, and other days I think I need to have things lined up."
>
> "This buys me some time to get ready."
>
> "Some days I can be calm and rational and think he's old and has to go sometime . . . and other days are just awful."

When the death of an animal companion approaches, we lose the confidence of knowing what can be predicted and planned for the future. "A time to lose" implies no longer being able to depend on all the daily interactions we've had and those aspects of our relationship we counted on. No longer does one's "taken for granted" world exist. Time and life feel fragile and tenuous.

It's a time of managing changes and living with changes—both those that are already known and those that are likely to come. Deepening feelings of sadness result from acknowledging the changes that are occurring and anticipating other changes. Time and life are significantly altered.

It's also a time of losing the ability to hold onto former decisions made about animals and their care as new clinical outcomes and observations become apparent. Decisions become harder because of availability of veterinary care and treatment possibilities. Doubts arise as people increasingly reconsider and ask, "Am I doing what's best for my animal right now?"

It can be a time of diminishing physical, emotional, and financial resources. Energy and strength may become depleted because of one's commitment to an animal's long-term care. One's role as caregiver and care partner may change as tasks of caregiving become more demanding. The ability to provide care over the long haul, while still maintaining other commitments, becomes increasingly limited. Ongoing nights of sleep deprivation, while meeting other responsibilities, can result in thoughts that one can't handle many more nights like that. To sustain and maintain the level of care that's required is exhausting. Additionally, ongoing veterinary expenses may deplete financial resources. To continue may not be possible.

This is a time to gather resources to help balance the losses: practical resources such as friends and family, veterinarians, information and coping resources, such as spirituality. It's a time to resolve to make decisions regarding treatment choices and options, a time to generate confidence in the clinical results of tests and treatments, a time to gain fortitude to do what needs to be done for one's animal, a time to establish commitment to one's own self-care, a time to develop the courage and compassion to say, "It's time," a time to make decisions about an animal's body after death, and a time to consider having rituals and memorials before and after the animal's passing.

While this time period is challenging and frequently overwhelming, it's clearly a time of profound devotion and love. It's a true witness to the depth of fidelity and commitment people have made to their animal companions. Erica summed this up:

If all I wanted were fairy tales and happy little sunshiny things, I would've gotten a stuffed animal. But I was willing to accept the vomiting, the diarrhea, the getting bitten and scratched. I was willing to accept the whole package when I decided to get a cat—the good and the bad.

ACKNOWLEDGING THE CHANGES

One of the key indications that people have entered into this time period of "getting ready" is their recognition of the changes in their animals, sometimes physical, other times mental or behavioral. Expressions such as "I know our time is limited" are common.

Sometimes the changes are gradual. Beloved animals slow down, sleep more, breathe more laboriously, eat less, have increasing incontinence, struggle up and down steps, appear weaker, lose weight, play less often, make different types of noises, bump into things, become more restless, move more stiffly, decrease activities, and look more uncomfortable. Pet parents see their animals aging, declining, or failing, and their hearts ache because of the changes. Sometimes part of the heartbreak is due to the grace, dignity, and courage with which their animal companions handle their aging and illness.

Debra recognized the changes in her cocker spaniel:

> Christmas the year before was when it really hit me. I could see that things were changing. While watching *101 Dalmatians* and seeing the puppies and the whole cycle of life, I started to get what the vet had been telling me. It was starting to sink in that Addison's thyroid was failing, his heart was enlarged, his eyesight was going, his hearing was failing, and he was sleeping more soundly. It just all hit me. I couldn't stop crying.

For some, the handwriting on the wall is not that clear. Sometimes it is only in retrospect that a person recognizes that a specific new symptom was actually the beginning of the end.

Others see more abrupt and immediate changes because of rapidly developing illnesses—vomiting, diarrhea, profound weakness and collapsing, disorientation, inability to eat and drink, dehydration, bloody stools, or seizures—brought on from injury, disease, infection, or organ or multi-system failure. Diagnostic test results come back and indicate major impairment. It's gut-wrenching to see one's animal living with these clinical problems.

Today Sarah, my fourteen-year-old dog, is back under the covers sleeping, and it's almost 11:00 A.M. She hasn't gotten up for breakfast yet, and she's making no moves to do so. I'm so mindful that Sarah has aged and that my time with her is limited. I see the changes even though I don't want to see them. They are still relatively small, and her quality of life is still good. There are times she still has bursts of energy. Yet I know the changes are there. Betty, my niece, noticed them when she visited last month. It had been three months since she had seen Sarah. Sarah didn't hear her come in, and Sarah had slowed down. I wanted her to say, "Oh, no, Auntie, she hasn't changed." Instead, she said, "Yes, I noticed that."

Now and then some pet parents acknowledge that they notice the changes but are reluctant to look at them earnestly.

GETTING READY

This time of "getting ready," with its uncertainty and unpredictability, is filled with challenges. In anticipatory grief a person grieves before a loss actually occurs. Is it possible to get ready emotionally and prepare for a companion animal's death? And if so, what's involved in this process? How does one maintain hope but not be in denial?

Debra started getting ready in December as she told Addison how much she loved him and how important he was to her. As his health continued to deteriorate, she said:

> I shifted gears. I knew things were happening, and I needed to get ready. I didn't want this to be happening, but I had no control over it. I went into work and told people I was afraid he was going to die soon, and I just sobbed. I think it was the saying it out loud that made the difference.

For Steve, getting ready meant trying every possible option. He described the two-month roller coaster ride from the time he got the positive test result until he made the agonizing decision to euthanize Porkchop. He recounted the ups and downs when one veterinarian would say there was hope and another would say there wasn't.

Kerry described her earlier experiences of getting ready, based on the care she had given her former cats:

> As horrible as it is, when you go through the illness with them, even though you're providing these interventions, you know they're on their way out. You know you're not going to have what you had before. You're trying to do whatever you're trying to do, but there's some place inside that knows these are remedial activities, at best. The whole time, even though you're not aware of it, emotionally you are getting prepared. So when it happens, you've got this sense that you did all you could, but it wasn't meant to be. When you've done everything and it's her time, you're more able to be okay.

Rob referred to this time of getting ready as his opportunity to consider the possibility of life without his dog, Zomax. As hard as it was to consider life without her, it would have been infinitely worse if he hadn't had this time:

> Both Zomax and I knew I was there for her. I'm pleased I was conscious of that while she was alive. I conveyed to her that she was extremely important to me and much loved. And as much as an animal can appreciate that, I think she did, and I felt it back.

On the other hand, others say it's not possible to get ready. "I think what you do, in fairness to them, as much as for your own hope, is you keep fighting," said Sharron. "And if you keep fighting, you can't get ready. They're mutually contradictory."

Patricia's voice also reflected an inability to get ready:

> I really thought I was prepared for my dog, Auggie's, death. I really didn't think I would react the way I did and certainly not for the length of time I have. People say nothing can prepare

you. I feel that way about Auggie passing away. I thought I was prepared, but I was wrong. I was way off target.

Sharron compared the difference in talking about getting ready and actually getting ready:

> I think you talk about it, but I don't think you really do it. I had talked about her being old and knowing I was going to lose her, that she couldn't live forever. But I don't think you really go there until you have to. You think you are, but they're just words. You just don't let go until you have to, and unless you can let go, you can't really prepare yourself.

Sometimes I think I do with Sarah what Sharron described. I say words like, "She's getting old," "I see the changes, " and "I know my time with her is limited." I want to be with her as much as I can. I'm aware how frequently I feel tenderness and sadness as I reflect on my deep love for her, all she means to me, and how much I'll miss her. Every day I thank her for being in my life and tell her how much I love her. But am I really getting ready emotionally? Or am I just saying the words? It's probably the latter.

Another dimension of getting ready is helping one's animal get ready. Pali talked with Leadbelly, her dog, telling him what a good friend he'd been to her and reminiscing with him about their life together—the good, the bad, and the funny. She described the importance of letting him know she'd be okay when he went. She also talked to her other animal companions. To Muddy Waters she said, "Are you going to be okay when Leadbelly is gone? What are we going to do when Leadbelly isn't here?" Pali believes that people deal with their own grief before an animal dies but that animals don't understand what's happening because people don't talk to them. The animal knows its guardian is sad and feels somewhat responsible because of its inability to comfort the person. "Animals have a much deeper understanding of all these emotions than people ever could," Pali says.

A dimension of Natalie's getting ready was her longing to have a healing ritual for her sixteen-year-old dog, Samantha. Samantha had been ill for almost a month and was showing only minimal improvement. While acknowledging the very real possibility of letting Samantha go, Natalie still wanted to prolong her life as long as humanely possible. Jack, a gentle and spiritual man, offered to hold a healing service for Samantha. I was invited to participate.

Jack lovingly and reverently held and looked into Samantha's face as he prayed aloud for her. Additionally, he read particular passages and stories of healing from a book on Jewish mysticism. Jack had heard that the Talmud teaches that one could change one's fate by changing one's name. Our prayer was that Samantha could be restored to renewed health. Samantha was given her new name, "Irene." From then on, we called her "Samantha Irene." Following the re-naming ritual, Jack led us in a laying-on-of-hands.

There was a sense in each of us that we had been part of an important spiritual moment. Natalie particularly described the solace and comfort she experienced from having offered such love and reverence to Samantha Irene. The memory and image of Samantha Irene looking up into Jack's face as he spoke to her and prayed for her is a memory Natalie still cherishes.

GETTING THE NEWS

Getting the news of an animal's failing health often is a critical time in the series of decisions that have to be made. Erica spoke of this regarding Mao:

> When I got the diagnosis, it was devastating. My vet said the C word, he said "cancer," and I started crying after I got off the phone. He was kind of guarded, but he didn't say there's nothing we can do. He said we had several treatment options we could try. I thought, "Okay, we have a plan, it's worth a shot," and even so, after I got off the phone, I burst into tears.

When Steve got the results of Porkchop's test indicating a highly infectious, incurable bacterial bird disease, he was encouraged to bring her in immediately for euthanasia. That was inconceivable. Instead, he had a good cry. Later he took Porkchop in for more tests, hoping for some treatment options.

In contrast, Jyl had little to no time after she got the news. She described the previous weeks as "crazy-making." She knew intuitively that Muffy, her cat, was dying. Yet she felt the veterinarian ignored her opinion by stating that Muffy could be treated. It was a Friday afternoon at 5:45 P.M. when the results came back. Muffy had an aggressive form of cancer with a poor prognosis:

> I had no idea she was going to die on that day in that way. I got the diagnosis that she had mammary cancer, and minutes later we're putting her to sleep. I had no time to get ready, no time to do anything.

WEIGHING THE DECISIONS

Usually there's a series of decisions to be made about treatment options. In the face of deteriorating health, we frequently have the ability to extend our animals' lives by the choices we make. With the range and extent of veterinary treatment options available today, the decisions related to treatment and caregiving become increasingly difficult. Huge questions and doubts arise over whether these treatments should be initiated. There can be a fairly high level of risk involved with certain diagnostic procedures. How does one weigh the risk-benefits ratio? There is the continuous and overriding consideration of quality of life versus quantity of life. There's the dilemma of extending life by treatment and care while not compromising the desired quality of life. Indeed, if life can be extended, what will be the cost—to the animal, the person, their shared life? When does it become too much? How do people know if they are letting their companion go too soon? Does the animal still want to keep going? How can anyone possibly know?

Some are able to remember the exact time they gave up the idea that their animal would get well. They came to realize and accept that things weren't going to get better. This acceptance became the cornerstone on which they made subsequent treatment decisions.

It's not unusual to set markers denoting when it will be "time to stop." Examples of such benchmarks are, "When my animal has more and more accidents in the house" or "When she can't get up without someone helping her," or "When he has more bad days than good days." Sometimes these markers stand and guide decisions. Other times adaptations are made and the benchmarks are modified, allowing people to provide care and treatment a bit longer. Later they reassess and, perhaps, set another touchstone.

Personal values and spiritual beliefs often underlie the treatment decisions made. The devotion that's been present between pet parents and their animal companions continues as a guiding force. Erica spoke of her decisions regarding Mao:

> The whole time I was attending Mao during his illness, I always reviewed my sense of values before I made every decision on what to do next. That meant that many times I wound up foregoing the easy way and made considerable sacrifices in order to do the right thing for Mao. I was never tempted to leave him in the lurch, because I was too tired or too broke, or too hungry or confused, or too busy or grief-stricken or too scared. I summoned all my will power, took a deep breath, held my head up and forged ahead. There were moments when it was excruciating to do so, but I did so anyway.

Rob struggled with the decision about initiating chemotherapy for his dog, Zomax:

> If you do it at Davis [School of Veterinary Medicine, University of California at Davis], they have pretty much everything, but

it's two-and-a-half hours up there. It's a whole day to do it that way. If you do it locally, you have to bring her in the day before to get the blood work done so they can target the chemo. Then she has to return the next day. So even if all goes well, she will have at least a day or two of not feeling good. So we've got three to four days a week not being so great in order to get another three that are maybe okay but maybe not. I was leaning against that. That wasn't the nicest quality of life for her.

During this time the central, often conflicting, role of veterinarians is magnified. People may work with several veterinarians with differing opinions, veterinary specialists, or a team of veterinarians at a major medical center. Sometimes a more holistic, complementary natural approach is encouraged.

Pet guardians often rely on veterinarians' expertise to provide a reality check, or a "read," as to whether it's appropriate to pursue further treatment. They look to their veterinarians to give them definite indicators to guide their decisions. Rob recalled how he was more bleak than his veterinarian who said, "Don't bury her before she's dead. There are still things we can do." Sometimes the veterinarian encourages further treatment, other times the pet guardian is the one to choose additional options.

Quality of life is a prevailing consideration. The degree of intrusiveness, amount of risk, possible pain, side effects, and the potential to impact the outcome affect treatment decisions. Because side effects of one approach can negatively impact other ongoing health problems, pet parents and their veterinarians have to weigh one decision against another. Sometimes past decisions about previous animals' care factor into the present decision-making process. Often, I've been told, "After what I did before, I don't want to do that now. I learned my lesson. I won't put this animal through that." Or I've heard, "I didn't fight hard enough the first time. I got scared and didn't think I could go on. This time I'm going to try a little longer and go for a second opinion if necessary."

People continually seek additional information to make informed decisions. How does one make sense of all the input and weigh all the options, which are sometimes contradictory? How much specific information about detailed pros and cons is needed to help one make an informed decision? How much additional time will a particular treatment give, especially if the possibility of remission is low? What are the success rates of the recommended treatments? Which veterinary recommendations does one accept and which does one challenge? When veterinarians themselves disagree on the most appropriate approach, the decision sometimes feels impossible and tentative. When one veterinarian recommends a particular approach and another says, "if you do, that can kill him," how do pet parents make the decisions? Do they go with the "Western" more traditional veterinary approach or choose the alternative, holistic treatments? Do they integrate both?

Living with such ambiguity and opposing views intensifies owners' stress levels. They want the necessary time to make the right decisions, but by taking the time, they know they may prevent the recommended treatment from maximizing its outcome. Time marches on while people struggle with decisions. There are times when inaction, no matter how well intentioned, results in unexpected, undesired outcomes. In these situations, individuals live regretfully with the consequences.

Pet parents take their caregiving responsibility seriously. They have the primary role of advocacy and decision-making for their pets. They want their animals' highest good. But how much and how long do they continue to advocate? Some see an animal's body as failing but feel the spirit as still healthy. Others experience a pet's spirit as preparing or ready to leave.

"We've got to find a way" reflects the continual pursuit of every possible reasonable treatment. Typically individuals want to know they did all they could for their animal if there was any ray of hope that the outcome might be improved. They sought experimental treatments if the life could be extended. They tried another medication if it looked promising. They traveled to another treatment facility, such as a major veterinary medical center, for second opinions—often at considerable cost, effort, and sacrifice. They sought out specialty veterinarians for another perspective if the quality and length of life could be enhanced.

Steve had to be absolutely sure he had tried everything. He wanted to give Porkchop, his parrot, every chance, even if there was only a little bit of hope. She was in his care, and he felt the responsibility. "I had to have a clear conscience, knowing I did everything," he said. "So there wouldn't be any, 'Well, what if . . .' I didn't want to live with that."

Sharron, too, needed that last week to know she had done all she could for her dog. But, with hindsight, Sharron thinks the week was a sad one of unnecessary struggling for both of them:

> I think I knew a week before I put her to sleep that she was in big trouble. It could have turned around though, so you don't know. They're tough calls. You just try everything you can, short of seeing your animal suffer unnecessarily. And as long as it was doable, I would have done it.

Ilana knew Cris Kitty wasn't going to survive because of his critical injuries from the fire:

> For us it was a question of whether we should put him to sleep at this point. Should we give him every chance, and if he pulls through, is he going to suffer and be sick the rest of his life? Knowing all the problems that were going on in his body, I couldn't imagine how he would be able to cope if he survived.

Yet Ilana said Elaine, Cris Kitty's other pet mom, needed to give Cris Kitty every opportunity. He'd previously survived another fire, and she believed he could make it again, "Elaine believes in miracles, and she needed to believe that this time, too, he might make it."

Debra, too, was willing to pursue whatever she needed to do for Addison:

> If it means giving him twenty meds a day, I'm going to do that. I remember praying, "Please let this work for as long as possible. Let the meds work the way they're supposed to. I'll do whatever it takes to keep him with me. Don't let him go yet."

The pursuit of every possible reasonable treatment can take a major toll. The caregiving tasks and level of care required are clearly demanding, as evidenced by Erica's care of Mao:

> After the first three weeks, things could have gone either way, but the second three weeks, he took a turn. His entire intestinal tract was affected by this cancer. He couldn't eat and got weaker and weaker. I had to bring him to the vet's office every single day for his chemo. So we made the daily pilgrimage. That was hard on him and on me. It was physically, emotionally, and financially exhausting for me. But I vowed that no matter how hard it was for me, I would take care of him first and make sure that he had whatever he needed for the day.

In Natalie's care of Samantha Irene, she, too, personified committed intense caregiving and love—she would work all day, arrange for mid-day caregivers, come home to the evening caregiver role, and fall into bed exhausted. Natalie made a bed for herself on the floor next to Samantha. Not only did this allow them to be close to each other, but Natalie was also able to check on Samantha and provide any needed care during the night. Then, in a few hours Natalie had to get up early to provide care—food, medicines, hydration, bedding changes, repositioning—before going to work. At the outset Natalie felt she could sustain Samantha Irene's caregiving for only a week or two. Yet as each week passed, Natalie extended her line in the sand a bit more as Samantha continued to improve.

Not everyone is able to handle such an enormous, ongoing responsibility. There may be no one with whom to share this caregiver role. The needed care is unmanageable and exhausting. This is particularly true when other demands are pressing. Other family members may need help and care. Or the pet guardians are working, and the animal needs a continuous level of care while they are away. Perhaps the animal is large and needs to be carried up and down the steps, and the person is physically unable to do so.

The ongoing and overwhelming burden of continuous caregiving is real and substantial, but it does not negate the love and commitment people have for their animal companions. It does not deny their deep-seated wish and desire to continue providing the necessary care. It is simply the reality of finite time, energy and resources: "I can do it for a week, but I'd never be able to manage this for a month." One can arrange for friends and family to help for short periods of time, but these persons, too, are limited in their ability to assist on a long-term basis.

My experience has shown me there is a very real need for a service that provides home care for pets—hospice care that is both long term and short term. Some who cannot sustain the required level of care feel they've failed their pets, and their resulting guilt and regret impact their grief.

EXPENDITURES

Expense is another realistic and practical limitation. Veterinary care can run into the hundreds and thousands of dollars. Specialty veterinary care can be quite expensive. Chemotherapy and radiation are costly. The expense of surgery and post-operative care can be prohibitive. Some people have the financial resources to incur the costs; others don't. Some go into debt, which they continue to pay off long after the animal has died. Erica experienced this:

> Thank goodness for credit cards. I said, "I'll deal with it later.
> I'll just spend a long time paying it off in small minimum

payment installments." And then I just accepted, hey, that's the way this hand is going to play itself out. I'm not going to rage against it. That's just part of the experience.

Others are unable to consider undertaking such an imposing debt. Some may be students who may not have the resources. Others need the money for other family obligations. Single people don't have anyone to help share the expense. For those who are unable to provide veterinary treatment because of financial reasons, the burden of guilt can be overwhelming and the regret especially strong. Through tears, they acknowledge how unfair it feels that they can't provide the necessary care to their animals due to limited financial resources.

Yet, I know with absolute conviction that to be unable to continue treatment because of financial reasons in no way negates the love and devotion that a person has for a loved animal. Instead, it reflects a genuine, practical, reasonable, and legitimate economic limitation.

POWERLESSNESS OVER OUTCOME

A frequently described emotion is powerlessness over the outcome: "There was nothing I could do about it." Treatment regimens and surgical procedures had been unsuccessful. There was the realization that one was doing everything one could, yet the animal wasn't getting better. No matter what the person did, what decisions were made, or what treatments were implemented, the sense of impotence was overwhelming.

Kerry referred to this perception as there being a bigger power, "something bigger in life than you; you logically know you can't change the outcome, there's something bigger than you."

Erica's journal entries of Mao's last few days reflect his vulnerability and her experience of helplessness:

That was the worst part—being helpless while he was dying. There was nothing I could do to reverse his illness or even arrest the progress of his illness. Everything else I had always done was so powerful for him—nourishing food, filtered tap water, good supplements, all my love—but when it came right down to the wire, I didn't have the power to change the final outcome. I felt I went face first into a wall. It was the only time I'd felt that kind of powerlessness in our relationship, and it was very frustrating.

Using metaphorical language to convey this experience of futility, Erica said:

In some ways I felt like I was standing on the beach when a tsunami warning had been issued. Even though I couldn't see it, I knew this big tidal wave was heading our way, and it was going to hit at some point. I knew it. I couldn't see it, but there we were on the beach. It was coming, and there was nothing I could do about it.

Jody felt totally incapable of easing Kasha's confusion:

I could tell she wasn't happy about the situation, but she was trying to deal with it. It was really hard to see how she wasn't able to do what she wanted to do, to get up and walk. We took care of her needs, but her confusion got to me most. She didn't understand, she was like a baby. They know they don't feel right and can't do certain things. That broke my heart because I couldn't make her understand.

Ilana's sense of loss of control and helplessness was described in more general terms. Her overall perception of safety had disappeared because of the fire. "I thought about all we do to protect our pets," she said. "In spite of all these measures, some things are just out of our control."

"IT WAS TIME"—EUTHANASIA
Is euthanasia an option? Can I do it? Is that what's best for my pet? What right do I have to play God and make that decision?

What do I look for to know it's the right time? How will I know if I'm doing it too soon or too late? Will I be able to be there and hold my animal? How can I make it easiest for my pet?

"It was time." Some people can say that with conviction and have minimal regret about their decision to euthanize. They knew "it was time." There was no hope for improvement. Others agonize while making the decision. Many live with major regrets and deep guilt afterward.

How do people make that decision for their animal companions, who often represent the most significant relationships in their lives? How do they know it is the right decision when they want desperately to do what is best for their beloved pet, who is trusting them completely?

"You'll know."   "But will I?"
"He'll let you know."   "But will he?"
"You won't miss it."   "But what if I do?"

This period of time is unique to the experience of pet loss. Most of us have limited, if any, previous experience with deciding to take a beloved pet's life.

Pet parents describe their monumental struggles with euthanasia and their repulsion of "playing God." "That's the hardest thing I've ever had to do" is a frequently made statement. They want to be sure.

For Debra, there came a time when she realized she and Addison's veterinarian had tried everything, and Addison couldn't go on any longer. "It helped me to tell my friends, 'It was time,'" she said. "Even though he was on many medications, his heart and lungs were giving out. He was drowning in his secretions. He wasn't eating, and he wasn't sleeping."

Still Debra voiced her ambivalence:

I think it was a gift I was able to give him to put him out of his pain. I do feel that way, but I remember having doubts during it, wondering if it was really the right time. I knew that it was, but I just wanted to be so sure, because my life was never going to be the same after that.

Attentiveness and hypervigilance result in being attuned to companion animals and sensing what they need. The exquisite degree to which individuals are sensitive to their animals results in observations that guide their decisions. They regularly say they're told by others that they'll "know." "Trust me, you'll know," and most say they do. The time comes when there is a noticeable difference, and a person just knows, "It's time now." They know this decision is the most merciful and compassionate step they can take.

Erica described how she knew it was time to let Mao go:

Once in a while I think about that last day and how hard it was, and sometimes it seems too painful to think about. But other times I want to remember how special his last day was. The day I had to euthanize Mao he'd given up the fight. He was a fighter through the whole thing. He was trying so hard and then, there was one day where I could actually see it in him: he just quit. I could actually see it in his whole vibe and body language. He just started to go somewhere else. There was no point in trying to keep him alive anymore.

I'm Ready to Go
Enough, please, I'm ready to go.
You've done all you can possibly do,
 and it's okay to let me go now.
You've always had my well-being foremost in your mind,
And I've known that.
You've always tended to my safety, and I've known that.
I thank you for all that you have done—
You've sacrificed sleep and rest—for me.
You've sacrificed your personal life—for me.
You've sacrificed your financial comfort—for me.

How could I ever doubt your love for me?
I couldn't, and I don't.
I never have before, and I don't now.
And, now, I thank you for what you are about to do.
You are going to let me go lovingly and unselfishly—
Neither of us is the same as we were
    before we adopted each other.
We've become part of the tapestry of each other's life.
Now wrap me lovingly in your love and hold me gently.
I will be part of your life's tapestry forever.
    —*Betty J. Carmack*

For Steve it didn't seem fair to leave Porkchop, his parrot, in isolation at the hospital any longer. The veterinarians all agreed there was no treatment for avian mycobacterium, a highly infectious organism. Getting a final diagnosis would be severely intrusive, requiring a biopsy, and necessitating her staying in isolation another two weeks. Increased exposure to the particular strain of mycobacterium would most likely compromise his own health even more. Additionally, there was a potential public health problem because of possible mutation of the mycobacterium. Unless a post-mortem was done, there would be no way to tell if the organism had been eliminated from her body. Because he wouldn't feel comfortable giving away a bird that could compromise someone else's health, and because she would eventually become quite ill, Steve agonizingly made the appointment for euthanasia, the most humane decision he felt he could make. He felt he was left with no other option.

While some pet guardians feel they know when "it's time," others don't. They agonize over when to do it. To do it too soon can feel like murder, yet, they abhor the idea of their animal suffering. They pray for the ability to discern how to make the right decision at the right time. They pray for their animal to give them a sign. While some feel they receive that sign, others don't. Because an animal's health is rapidly deteriorating, some people set the appointment for a particular day and time, fully expecting to implement their decision. Yet that morning their animal is unexpectedly better, and the appointment gets cancelled. The ups and downs of the roller coaster ride continue. For some, this scenario happens more than once, and the confusion, turmoil, and vulnerability continue.

Some people feel guilty because they "did it too soon." They thought they let their animal go before the pet was really ready, or the decision was made more for their benefit than the animal's. The person was understandably exhausted and couldn't bear seeing the animal suffer any longer.

Others feel guilty because they "did it too late." They think their animal went on too long and suffered more than necessary. They feel they should have decided a few days or weeks earlier. Sharron felt this way:

> I hate myself now for the two weeks that Gigi was sick and the discomfort she felt. I still wish she hadn't had to go through that. I hated leaving her home. I worried. If I'd come home and found her dead, I would have hated myself for not being with her. There is no right decision. No matter what you do, you don't win on that one.

Thirteen years ago, I felt it was the right decision at that time for Sunshine, my cocker spaniel. In consultation with her veterinarian, I waited one more day so he could examine her, anesthetized, to explore what was happening inside her ear. If something could be "fixed" within a fairly short period of time so she'd regain a reasonably good quality of life, I would consider treatment. However, if the results of the examination showed a poor prognosis for regaining any decency of life, I would let her go without bringing her back to consciousness.

I was giving permission to let my dear Sunshine go. Yet, in my heart of hearts I knew that was the most compassionate and loving gift I could offer her. She was pitiful from the neurological involvement. It broke my heart to see her staggering around, unable to stand, eat, or drink. I'm not sure she even knew I was there. I couldn't tell if she was seeking me out or not. What she was feeling could not have been good. She had no quality of life at that point, although I don't think she was in physical pain. Had she been, I would have let her go immediately.

Waiting one more day to have the exam done was part of my need to be sure. I knew I would miss her terribly, but I also knew with conviction that she wouldn't want to live like that. In my value system, that was not quality of life. Euthanasia was something I could do *for* Sunshine, not something I was doing *to* her. Blessedly, I felt then, as I still do, that euthanasia was a merciful gift to her.

LIVING DURING THIS TIME

"Is he okay today?" Every day with an ailing animal is significantly altered from regular life. There's an increased focus, concentration, hypervigilance, and engagement—always on alert, watching for evidence that something different is happening, observing for signs of deterioration and discomfort, indications that the pet needs something additional or new. One is never sure what a day will be like.

This increased awareness is often accompanied by heightened, even overwhelming, emotions. This period is occasionally depicted as feeling like "a time bomb waiting to go off." Some describe their feelings as increasingly present, visible, accessible, and intense. Erica described it this way:

> My own adrenaline was buzzing, and I had a lot of physical and emotional energy. All my emotions were turned up a few notches, so everything was charged up a little bit. I was right there.

In contrast, others have to suppress their feelings in order to be strong for their animals. They don't want their emotions to get in the way of their ability to assess their animals' needs and recognize their required responses.

Uncertainty can result in a perception that today or tomorrow could be an animal companion's last day. Living each day on the brink of death changes a person's perspective and consciousness. Erica continued:

> I lived every day as if it was my last with him. I actually postponed taking a day trip to the East Bay Hills because I thought, "Today could be the day that Mao dies, and if I'm not here, he's all alone. The hills, though, will still be there, so they can wait."

Life is not the same. With the unpredictability, it's impossible to live one's life as one had previously. Different choices are made. Former life patterns no longer work. People become detached from the normal daily routine and all the seemingly mundane things that go on. It's a strange place to be in and still try to live the rest of one's usual life. Natalie said, "While Samantha Irene is still here, other things simply don't happen."

This period feels like a time of waiting—waiting to see if the animal will respond to a new treatment, waiting for the results of diagnostic work, waiting for the veterinarian to return a call, waiting to see if the pet is better tomorrow, waiting until the regular veterinarian gets back, or waiting for death, either by euthanasia or by natural means. For some, like Steve, the waiting was brutal:

> Just waiting . . . I mean how do you pick a date to put your companion to sleep? I called and immediately started crying. They said, "Tomorrow?" And I said, "Tomorrow's too soon." So I made an appointment for a week. I specifically set some time aside each day just to be with her. The getting ready for me was exhausting every possibility. Now there was just waiting.

During this time period there's also a sense of fighting that's reflected in the figurative language used, "We're fighting the war on cancer," and "He is a real little fighter," or "We won that last battle, but now we have a new one." Unfortunately, however, the words and phrases often reflect disappointing outcomes: "Even though I fought and fought for him, we lost," or "He lost his war on cancer; he had fought so hard, but he lost." "She gave up the fight" and "He fought so long and hard, and it broke my heart to see him lose his battle" reflect an animal's inability to keep going.

Chris shared with me an experience she had when Mavis, her ten-year-old bearded collie mix, was no longer able to go on their shared walks because of her cancer. On one of Chris's solo walks, out of a place unseen, a golden retriever wagging her tail excitedly, ran up to greet Chris. When Chris saw this dog looking at her, she felt strongly that this was Gaelen, her sister's golden retriever, who had been Mavis's good friend. Gaelen had passed away a year ago. Chris felt this dog had come momentarily to let her know everything would be alright and not to worry about Mavis. For Chris, this animal's greeting brought her comfort for the next several weeks. She has never forgotten it.

There's a mindfulness of, and a responsiveness to, an animal's most basic needs. Individuals' loving care of their companions reflects their strongly held value of, and belief in, commitment. Animals' heads are supported to help them eat as they're encouraged to lick water and food from pet parents' hands and fingers. Bedding is frequently changed because of incontinence. Harnesses and straps are used to help animals stand and walk. Animal companions need intensified 'round-the-clock care. This degree of unselfish care reflects a deep devotion to an animal. Rachel experienced this first hand with Kasha:

> Getting through that last two weeks, it felt like a doggie hospice. I realized when I was carrying Kasha [her thirteen-year-old Airedale] up and down that I had gotten into a rhythm where my life focused around working and coming up and checking on her and making her comfortable. That's all that counted.

The covenant made long ago continues.

SAYING GOOD-BYE

Saying good-bye occurs in different ways. Often, there's a series of good-byes as one acknowledges successive changes and losses in an animal's health requiring modifications in the life previously shared. There's also a sense of savoring the preciousness of the limited time that's left. Rachel spoke of this:

> That time becomes precious, just being with her, being close to her, that's what helped me get through it. That's what I do, that's what helps me, it's just the right thing to do. Even though there wasn't much I could do for her, I wanted to be around her—to sit with her. She wasn't all that comfortable, it was hard for her to breathe. I'd gently touch her. Sometimes I don't even know if she wanted to be touched. One of the ways I dealt with it was sitting here and communing with her and telling her I loved her. There wasn't anything else I could do.

The good-byes are often conscious and purposeful. They can also be heartbreaking. Rob experienced this with his English bulldog:

> I literally told Zomax how much I loved her, and how much I was going to miss her. That was pretty gut-wrenching for me. As hard as it's been, it would be much worse if I hadn't had the time to entertain the possibility of life without her.

This time of saying good-bye is reflected in the many tender ways people choose to be present to their pets. The extent to which people go is both impressive and touching. As I hear their stories, I'm again reminded of the Prayer of St. Francis, ". . . it is in giving that we receive . . ."

There is a strong desire to do more for their animal companions during the remaining time. Pet parents note their very real commitment to love their animals as best they can until the very end. Importantly, time is made for their pets—time simply to be with an animal. Rob told of spending this time with Zomax:

I had maybe two weeks when it was fairly clear that, without a major miracle, she would die pretty soon. And one of the things that I elected to do was spend as much time with her as I could to try and make her final days special. I took her to new places in the car because she liked to ride in the car. It was really very noticeable when you took her someplace new, just to watch her face, and see her sniff things.

After their much-loved dog Barclay's diagnosis, and while he was still feeling good enough to enjoy the trip, Barry and Carolyn took him back to Hope Valley, a place they had gone as a family every fall. With trails to hike, and a river in which to swim, Barclay had always loved this place. Together as a family and treasuring their time together, this trip, though, was bittersweet. They knew they wouldn't be back again to Hope Valley with Barclay. On this trip Barclay was noticeably more tired and couldn't enjoy his previous level of hiking and swimming. Carolyn was in tears most of the weekend as she saw the physical changes in their beloved Barclay.

It's not uncommon for people to sleep with their pets on the floor during the last weeks or days of their lives. Debra said:

I didn't sleep on my bed because Addison couldn't get up there anymore. His heart and lungs were giving out. I had my arm on him, and I would stir if he would breathe heavily, wondering if I should give him more medicine. I kept wishing, when I drifted off to sleep, that I'd wake up and he would have died with my arm around him.

Elaine did the same with Pumpkin, her golden retriever, on her last night—lying on the floor with Pumpkin, giving her water out of her cupped hand, and looking into Pumpkin's eyes. Elaine treasures that tender memory of the preciousness of their time together.

. . . a time to lose . . .

Chapter 3

A Time to Let Go

"a time to die" (Eccles. 3:2)

I knew my life was changing and that things would never be the same. I also knew in my heart it was exactly what I needed to do, the best thing for him. It was really important to me that I could be there with him to say good-bye and be with him until the end. To say, "See? I kept my word. I promised you I would never leave you."
—*Debra*

"A time to die . . ." is when we accompany our beloved animal companions on the last of their earthly journey—an unparalleled role and responsibility. The decision to let go, sometimes having been agonizingly made, has to be implemented. Helping an animal pass over at the time of death is a critically decisive step that pet parents are called upon to take. To choose a time and a place to give one's pet over to death can feel unreal and unthinkable. This is the brutal one.

Behind the decision to accompany a loved animal on this final journey lies a great deal of dedication and love. As people talk of their animals' final days, hours, and minutes, their degree of commitment and devotion is obvious. Through their stories, I've heard their love both spoken and unspoken—whether the deaths were gradual and expected or sudden and unexpected. The enduring covenant is visible.

DYING OF NATURAL CAUSES

"I just hope God takes him while he's sleeping" or "I hope some morning she just doesn't wake up"—the notion of an animal dying of natural causes without outside intervention is a frequent hope. The idea of one's pet passing gently into the night while sleeping is preferred. The image of an animal dying quietly and peacefully at home with the pet parent present is comforting. When animals die naturally, it seems easier to accept.

Josie and Michael's little dog, Rose Kennedy, died peacefully in her sleep. When Michael called, "Come on Rosie, it's time to get up with Daddy," she lay there motionless. Similarly, Scott's fourteen-year-old beloved black Lab, Jackie, died in her sleep while lying on the floor with her head between her paws. The date was Valentine's Day, a day for Scott that will forever carry with it a memory of sadness.

The term, "natural causes," is curious to me. What does that actually mean? Aging, or elderliness, I think, is "natural." But is death by an illness still "natural"? The term tends to imply that a pet dies on its own without euthanasia or from an injury or acci- dent. But what about heart attacks and strokes? Are they "natural?" What's the line between "natural causes" and "unnatural causes"?

My experience with my dog Puccini's death was a totally different experience of death than Rocky's or Sunshine's. Her body actually gave out and she died. But naturally? No, I wouldn't call it natural, because pancreatitis, which showed up on the autopsy, killed her. But she died on her own as opposed to euthanasia or accidentally. She'd lived with a seizure disorder for several years, but this new illness—the one that took her life—wasn't related to her seizures. She'd been sick for a couple of days during Thanksgiving weekend, and I saw her getting progressively weaker. I'd taken her to the veterinarian on Saturday afternoon. He sent us home with some mild gastrointestinal medicine. Later, looking back, I think the clinical indications were there, but they were missed. By Sunday night, she was so weak she couldn't stand without my support. She wasn't eating or drinking fluids. She had no urine or stool output. Monday morning about 5:00 A.M. I woke up and looked at her, lying in my bed. I put her on the floor, and she couldn't stand, even with my help. I drove her to the emergency hospital. She was barely alive, if she even was alive, when I arrived. Sadly, within minutes she was gone.

I remember feeling shock and disbelief. I had known she was getting sicker and weaker, so on some level I was "getting ready." But on the other hand, I was in disbelief. What is the line between hope and denial? I was partially in denial about Puccini's condition. On one hand, by Sunday night I was contemplating the possibility of her dying, but on another, I wasn't. I still believed she could rally.

Choosing Euthanasia

Death by euthanasia presents its own unique challenges and struggles. There are different perceptions of euthanasia—something one *gives to* a pet, or something one *does to* a pet. How one views euthanasia—*doing for* versus *doing to*—can make a difference in the resulting experience of grief.

An animal becomes increasingly ill and needs help to release the suffering. One can't bear seeing one's pet struggling with this diminished quality of life. Or, a pet is the victim of an accident resulting in severe injuries, causing major pain and suffering. At those times, euthanasia is a merciful act of release—offering the gift of a gentle and graceful transition—no more suffering; no more struggling; no more pain.

The pet's family must decide who will be present at the time of euthanasia. Multiple factors impact this very individual decision. Some people want to be present to comfort, hold and talk with their animal at the time of death. On the other hand, others don't want that to be their last memory. They don't feel they can be sufficiently strong for their animal, and they fear their own emotions, such as anxiety and sadness, will make it harder for the pet.

Some persons don't know they have the option of being present and often feel regret and resentment later when they learn they could have been. The option wasn't offered to them, and they didn't know to ask.

Debra assured that gentleness and compassion were part of Addison's death:

> I was able to say to him, "You don't have to suffer any more. We're going to be with you. We're going to do this in a loving way. You don't have to hang on for us." My friends helped me have it in a way that was really caring and loving. I brought him to our vet and was with him at the time I chose to let him go. One friend had brought over a guardian angel candle, which I had been lighting for two nights and two days. We gathered his yellow blanket, his little teddy bear, and Squeaky Peas, his favorite toy, and we took them to the vet. Addison was able to walk down the front steps with his dignity. Our neighbors were standing on the front steps crying and waving good-bye to us. I couldn't even look at them. I sat in the back seat of my friend's car, holding Addison. When we got to the vet, we went back into the room and spread his yellow blanket on the floor with his candle, bear, and Squeaky Peas. The vet explained everything very gently and wonderfully. I had two good friends with me who were good friends of Addison's, too. We were with him on the floor. It was just so sad and so hard.
>
> Afterward, one of the things that was most comforting was that Addison looked like the puppy he was when I first got him. He looked so relaxed and at peace. All the muscles in his

face relaxed. He hadn't looked that way in a long time because he'd been laboring with his breathing. I buried my face in his fur, while my friends hugged me.

Steve tells of letting go of his parrot:

I was glad I was there. There's no other way I would have done it, but it was horrible. The vet was very compassionate. They wheeled Porkchop out on a cart because they have to have her unconscious to give her the barbiturates. There was a tube over her head so she could breathe in anesthesia, and I could see her face through the tube. Her cheeks were all blushed and pink. I helped hold her wing open so they could give her the barbiturates. It was just so sad. Everyone said I was doing the right thing, but I didn't feel like it. I had no other choice. Afterward, I just held her, weeping. I was glad Chuck [his friend] was there. He thought some of what I was putting myself through was so unnecessary. I reassured him that maybe it was, but I had to do it all.

Flowers were incorporated into the tender and loving way Chris let her dearly loved dog, Mavis, go. As she and her sister were sitting with Mavis in the sun on Mavis's last earthly day, Chris decided she wanted to send Mavis off with flowers. As they sat with Mavis, they made a garland of fresh deep red snapdragons and white chrysanthemums. Later that afternoon, Mavis died quietly and gently, and Chris lovingly and reverently placed the flowers around Mavis's neck. Mavis looked so peaceful and beautiful, and Chris's sister said, "Mavis looks like she's going to Hawaii." Their laughter intermingled with their tears.

Janet believes her eighteen-year-old poodle, Missy, guided them on her last day:

Missy always shook and was afraid of the vet, but on that day she lay cuddled in Tod's [her son] arms at peace. I believe she knew, and even as sick as she was, she helped us by not being afraid and showing us she was ready. It was her last gift to us—the knowledge we were doing the right and only thing even as the doctor administered the medicine—and she lay quietly. I held her little face in my hands and stared into her eyes, and she gazed right back until it was over.

Releasing her dog by euthanasia was an experience Sharron also had:

They said she was uncomfortable and not doing well. I said, "I'll come right over." As soon as I arrived, I could see she already had her little IV. I got to hold her in my arms while they injected her. The worst part was coming home alone. I didn't think I was going to make it. But you know, you do.

The choice of location where euthanasia occurs tends to be at the veterinary hospital. However, increasingly people request that their veterinarian come to their home. Sally and Larry did that for Paddy, their twelve-year-old Boston terrier, who drifted off in Sally's arms on the same bed she had slept in the night before—their bed.

Likewise, Gates, too, chose to have her nineteen-year-old cat, Blackie, die at home in their "Florida room," which overlooks the flower garden and yard. Gates was with Blackie all day and told him what they were doing. Blackie looked at her with a peacefulness she'd never before seen in him. Blackie accepted the veterinarian and offered no resistance. She and Bill, her husband, told Blackie how much joy he had given them. Gates held Blackie and saw his beautiful eyes close as her own tears ran down her cheeks onto his fur.

SUDDEN AND UNEXPECTED DEATHS

Sudden sorrow engulfs those persons whose animal companions die suddenly and unexpectedly. Something happens, and the pet's life is immediately in imminent danger. The animal instantly falls down—and dies. Or a pet seems well one morning and by evening has died—possibly from a heart attack, a stroke, or causes unknown. An animal is hit by a car and immediately, or soon after, dies. Disasters occur—fires, floods, earthquakes, tornadoes. Another animal or a malicious person attacks and kills. Pets disappear, some having been stolen. Some escape and run away, getting out of yards and doors. These types of unexpected losses and emergencies dramatically impact the grief experience. Profound challenges and difficulties accompany an abrupt death. Without time's cushion, grief's sting is all the more painful.

I've heard many heartbreaking stories of tragedies that have occurred. One of the lessons I've learned from these stories is that we do the best we can for our companion animals. We feed them good food, provide them with clean water, give them love and affection, and provide them with state-of-the-art veterinary care. We make every effort to keep them safe and well, but some things are outside our control.

Sudden, unexpected deaths are described, tearfully, painfully, angrily, haltingly, in both group and one-on-one counseling sessions. Each story is different, reflecting a particular context and set of circumstances. Yet, themes of total lack of preparation and shock run through each story. In the next few pages are stories of sudden loss and crushing sorrow.

Robert and Bonnie's beloved Basko, a German shepherd, died of heat stroke on a hike:

> It was a difficult walk going through brush. We all got up to a rock and stayed there twenty or thirty minutes. Basko stayed in the shade while we were there. Just before we got to the rock, Basko sort of nudged my hand. I didn't think much about it. I thought he wanted a drink of water. He just nudged my hand, which was something he would always do when I was working at my desk if he wanted something. I don't think I was sensitive to what he was telling me, "It's way too hot for me here."

So we took off. It was a very hard hike. Basko kept stopping in the shade. All of a sudden his rear legs seemed to give out, like he'd dislocated his hip or something. He sort of collapsed under a tree. We'd been giving him water to drink. There were never any signs of dehydration. I kept looking at his tongue for white coating. I gave him as much water as I gave myself. But when he collapsed under the tree, his eyes were open, and he didn't want to drink anymore. We thought his hips were dislocated and we'd have to carry him out of there. I decided to stay with him while the others hiked back down to get a blanket and the car.

When they got back, he was having severe breathing problems, and I knew he was dying. His breathing stopped before his heart stopped. Bonnie tried to ventilate him, but it was too late. It was only then that it dawned on me that he was having heat stroke. I'm pretty sure that the symptom of his legs collapsing was a symptom of heat stroke. He was dead. We all four carried him out.

Because of the absolute suddenness of Basko's death, Robert and Bonnie had no time to prepare. Additionally, Basko was only six years old, just halfway through his expected chronological life. He'd been in good health. That morning when Robert and Bonnie woke, they had no idea their Basko would be dead by the afternoon.

Robert recounted that because he didn't recognize the heat stroke for what it was, there was not a period of getting ready for Basko's death. He was thinking, instead, of how they would manage his hip dislocation—how to find a veterinarian, whether he'd need immediate surgery, whether they'd have to leave him at the veterinary hospital or be able to take him on home to their regular veterinarian. Several times during the hour of waiting for help, he'd go over to Basko, talk to him, kiss him, tell him that "Mommy will be back soon," and that they'd carry him out and take him to the doctor. The time between his realization that Basko was dying and the actual death was no more than a few minutes. He went on to say that had he recognized the heat stroke for what it was, he thinks he "would have gone crazy" because of his inability to have done anything to have changed the outcome. As he told me his story, he disclosed the personal torment that Basko's death had caused.

I could relate to his experience. His story brought my experience with Rocky right back. The absolute surprise of both deaths was similar. Just as Robert said he had no indication that Basko was dying, I had no clue that morning that Rocky would be gone. We each felt totally unprepared as each death was completely unexpected.

Likewise, Pali's tiny little bird, Bella, was a continual source of joy, dancing with Pali and flying around her. On one occasion, Bella had been on top of her birdcage when Pali went to get her some water. Bella flew down to the floor to be with Pali, when one of her hunting-type rescue dogs instinctively attacked Bella. Within seconds Bella died in Pali's arms:

> I was holding her to my chest, and I could feel her die. I knew the minute she died. I just felt a big vast space, and her tiny little being flew into me. I couldn't believe it. It was so quick, just seconds. There was nothing I could do, either. There was no rushing her to the vet. I was thankful to be holding her. I walked around sobbing and holding her. It was devastating. I couldn't handle it. I pictured her getting old with me.

For Ilana, it was a residential fire that took her loved animals:

> This was our worst nightmare. I got the call that the apartment had burned down, that Ian, our cat, was dead, and that Cris Kitty was in intensive care on a ventilator. Valerie and Hudson, both dogs, were also in intensive care. Seeing them all in the hospital, all at the same time, was surreal. I couldn't believe it was happening. I didn't even recognize Cris Kitty. They were young and healthy cats at the time. To have a fire felt so wrong. There was a point where it hit me: Cris Kitty was unconscious,

and his feet were wrapped. He had been burned. I was completely shocked. The trauma of it is hard to describe, it was just so much to absorb. These were like our children. Knowing they had been trapped in the apartment and thinking how frightened they must have been was one of the hardest psychological things with which we had to cope. Knowing Cris Kitty was dying, we prepared to let him go. But it didn't make it any less painful when he died. It was just as painful as Ian. Ian died suddenly. Actually it was less painful with Ian because it was quick. I know he suffered a very short time. Whereas with Cris Kitty, it was a question of what we should do.

Patricia, too, had to cope with the sudden, unexpected death of her dog:

I was tormented by the suddenness of Auggie's illness. One minute he's walking, and the next minute he's down. His breathing became labored. I was afraid I'd injure him. He's about fifty-five pounds. I was by myself. I was frantic to call for a pet ambulance.

I told him what a great dog he'd been and that he'd been my best pal. I sang to him. I called him all his names and nicknames. I went through "this is your life." "Remember the time we went to the beach." I told him about all the different foods he liked. I said, "This is just a dress rehearsal, I'm sure you'll be fine, but just in case, I want to make sure that you know this."

One of the things I remembered from a book was to be very reassuring to a pet who's passing away. Be very calm. Don't cry, because it will upset them. Give them permission to go. I was doing all those things. I told him I was okay now in my new marriage, and that he'd done his job well. I gave him permission to move on if he was tired.

I finally got a pet ambulance. By the time the woman came, he had a glazed look on his face. There was a slight pinkish color in his drool. I knew something had happened.

Something had burst. The woman said there was no place for me in the ambulance and it'd be better if I drove alongside. I felt like I should have been in the ambulance with him. The doctors said it was either a stroke or heart failure.

Elinor recounted the events surrounding the night Idgie, her cat, suddenly died. Elinor was utterly unprepared. At the time she didn't recognize he was dying, or that there was anything she should have done differently. Looking back, however, she had another perspective. It was as if he died of bad timing, because there were so many factors against him. Her exhaustion and hormonal imbalance and, ultimately, her inability to stay calm in the developing emergency when he stopped breathing, were the primary factors she cited:

> I completely lost it. I think it was because I loved him so much, and I was so fearful he was dying. It was something so far beyond my skills. I didn't know what to do. If I could have calmed down and gotten a grip on myself, I could have remembered CPR. I feel at fault because I wasn't able to help him because I hadn't taken care of myself, hadn't gotten enough sleep or eaten the right kinds of foods. There wasn't anything stacked in his favor for it to be tweaked so he could have lived. That, and the fact that I put my finger down his throat, I feel like I stopped his breathing. He was at the wrong place at the wrong time with the wrong problem.

Those persons who experience an unforeseen death frequently say that a week or so earlier they had been cognizant of, and enjoying, their pet's apparent good health. Thus, their surprise from a completely unexpected death is shocking.

FEELING SUPPORT
The compassionate presence of friends, family, and professionals makes a major difference at the time of an animal's passing. Debra was appreciative of her support network:

I have several friends, and we all made a pact. We'd all be there for each other for our pets, any time of the day or night. We could call. It took me a long time to hear that, to know that I didn't have to do it all by myself. My friends were here, and my neighbors were here. Addison's upstairs dog friend, Stella, came down to say good-bye, too.

When Mileva had Tribble, her cat, euthanized, her priest, Nedi, accompanied Mileva to the veterinarian's office. After Tribble's death, her veterinarian joined Mileva and Nedi in praying the Lord's Prayer.

Steve described how supportive he found people to be. His veterinarian reassured him that he was making the right decision because there was no treatment for Porkchop's illness. A friend, "a bird person whose birds are her babies," supported his decision, as did the friend's veterinarian. Yet, sometimes even with all the support received, it can be hard for individuals to believe they've done the right thing.

QUESTIONS AND GUILT ABOUT CIRCUMSTANCES

Questions, regrets, self-doubts and guilt can accompany deaths, whether they're natural, anticipated, planned, accidental, or unexpected. Certain contextual factors make the time for getting ready especially difficult, and often impossible. When a pet dies suddenly and unexpectedly from an accident or abrupt illness, or is stolen or runs away, people have three significant challenges. First, they must deal with the tragic manner of death; second, they feel cheated out of time to prepare; and third, they don't have a time to say good-bye. For pet guardians of young animals with whom they anticipated a long life, losing a pet at this age is incomprehensible. With unexpected deaths the questioning and recrimination are sometimes magnified, resulting in longer lasting guilt. Additionally, if the person feels responsible and guilty for the death, the depth of grief is exponentially increased. Robert acknowledged the regret and guilt he felt about Basko's death: "I feel really stupid about the whole thing. I just didn't think it was too hot."

Patricia used the word "tormented" to describe her questions and concerns over the way Auggie died:

It wasn't supposed to happen that August 1st night with the drama and the trauma. I had a little scenario in my head, and when it didn't play out that way, it really put me in a tailspin. I didn't think it was going to happen in a couple of hours. I thought he would gradually decline. He would ultimately be on medication and one day he would go to sleep and not wake up. It wouldn't be that one minute he's walking around, being his normal self, and within three hours, he's dead. I felt so powerless, helpless, and hopeless, all those things that I do everything in my power not to feel.

Additionally, there are other types of loss and death that present their own particular set of challenges and grief. When a relationship ends by divorce or separation, one person loses not only a spouse or partner, but a pet as well. The individual left behind can feel unbearably adrift and alone.

Especially difficult is when a young, physically healthy animal has to be euthanized or given away due to behavioral problems. Typically, it's a dog that's aggressive, and "something has to be done." The dog is threatening others, either in or outside the home. Sometimes those others are people, sometimes they are animals. Usually by the time the decision has been made to remove the dog from the home, the individuals involved have tried everything they know to do.

That happened to Tom, who told me his story of having to let go of Skye, "It was horrible, just horrible." Skye was the dog he'd had when he was single, and he said the two of them were quite close. Skye was so important to Tom and Michelle, his bride, that at their wedding Michelle had the groom's cake made in the likeness of a Jack Russell Terrier. When their son, Blake, was born, both Blake and Skye competed for Tom and Michelle's attention. Unfortunately, Skye nipped Blake. Wanting to keep Skye, Tom and Michelle tried behavioral techniques such as keeping Skye restricted to the bathroom. They planned to reintroduce Skye and Blake again, slowly. Regrettably, this reintroduction didn't go well, and there was another aggressive act. Tom and Michelle had to make the difficult decision to find another home for Skye.

While there was no doubt in their minds that this needed to be done, the thought of giving Skye away was wrenching. The decision and relocation needed to be done quickly. Because of the necessary suddenness, Tom questions whether he found the best home for her. After the adoption, a series of events raised concerns about the family that adopted her and their ability and willingness to provide the type of home and care he had wanted for her. These doubts and concerns gnawed at him, and after four years the outcome still isn't resolved for him. At some point, he said, he had to just let it go or it would eat him up.

Later there were times he considered contacting the veterinarian to inquire as to how Skye was. However, he knew he may have heard something he'd prefer not to have heard. He decided, "Sometimes with things like this, it's better to leave them alone." When Michelle or Blake speak now of getting a new pet, Tom says his first response is, "No way. We did that once, and it didn't work out." He is aware of his resistance to pursue that course and feels that getting another pet would not be fair to Skye.

This struggle of letting go of a physically healthy animal was also captured in the story that James Brewer-Calvert, pastor of First Christian Church, Decatur, Georgia, told me:

> One autumn afternoon I was correcting the spelling on the marquee sign on the church lawn. A young woman walked across the grass and asked if I was a priest. Between sobs she said, "I was raised Catholic and need a priest. The Catholic church across the street said their priest was out for the day. Are you one? I would like a priest to say last rites over my dog. Can you do that? Is it done for animals?" I said, "I am a pastor and would be honored to pray with you for your pet."

We walked toward the church parking lot. A young man was sitting in a new car with a large frisky rottweiler. The dog filled the back seat and drooled happily out the window. She said, "He is only two years old. There is nothing wrong with him physically, but he bit two dogs recently. I don't want him to bite a child. We're taking him to the vet at two o'clock to have him put to sleep. I don't know if we are doing the right thing, but I'm afraid he might hurt a kid. I thought maybe a priest could say a prayer over him. . . ." Her voice trailed off.

I invited the man and the dog to get out of the car. We knelt in a circle around the dog who alternated giving kisses and drool to the three faces now at his eye level. I said, "When you see your veterinarian ask her about alternatives," and I suggested questions for them to ask. "You are making a tough choice for the sake of the safety of children, and I admire your commitment to the welfare of your neighbors. As a father of young children allow me to say thank you for caring."

Then I said, "I believe the God who created and creates loves this dog, and whenever he passes away God will receive him into the Creator's loving embrace. Let's pray for the everlasting salvation of the soul of this beautiful dog, a pet who has brought much love into your lives and who may need to be put to sleep and sacrificed for the sake of other animals and children. Let's pray that you are never alone and are always in touch with the forgiving, nurturing grace of God. Let's pray for the strength and courage for the hour ahead of us." We bowed our heads and caressed the dog's back and ears as we prayed aloud and silently to a mighty Spirit who wept with us.

The sorrow in this story was counterbalanced by the sacredness of the moment—a sacred time and place created to bless this beloved family dog. Even though the dog most likely died that afternoon, the couple's life went on. They could hold forever their memory of blessing and saying good-bye to a dearly loved family member. With time and grace, perhaps, they came to an acceptance of their decision. The power of spirituality and prayer can transform anguish into peace.

Sometimes a death is somewhat easier to accept if an animal lives beyond its expected lifetime or if the death is perceived as something God willed or planned. Additionally, if people have tried every option available and done everything they could reasonably be expected to do, accepting a death can be somewhat less difficult. One's underlying theological beliefs can influence one's experience at this time because there are often theological issues or questions. Some people have the same theology of death for animal companions as they do for people. Others don't.

Spirituality can be a powerful resource and source of strength at this critical time of a loved animal's passing over—this time of significant transition. I offer this prayer, written for Sarah, to other pet parents who are lovingly helping their animals on this last step of their shared earthly journey.

Invocation

Come, Spirit, and be with her now as I give her back to you.
She has blessed my life in ways I never could have imagined.
She has loved with a pureness of love.
She has played with a passionate joy.
She has protected our home with a strong sense of purpose.
She has been the wind beneath my wings.
She has been the solid footing beneath my steps.
I will still feel her wind,
I will still feel her solid footing,
They are part of me forever.
As you gently take her to her next place in the circle of life,
Hold her, but not too tightly, for now's her time to step
    into peace and light.
    —Betty J. Carmack

. . a time to die . . .

Chapter 4

A Time to Grieve

"a time to weep . . . a time to mourn"
(Eccles. 3:4)

I fell apart. Even now I think about this, and I can't believe I'm still alive. I can't believe I didn't die of a broken heart. I would not ever want to feel like this again.
—*Patricia*

"A time to weep . . . a time to mourn" is the scriptural passage depicting this time of acute and ongoing grief, with its raw pain and intense sorrow that goes to the core of a person's soul. This is a time about suffering and giving oneself permission to grieve because of the profound absence of an animal companion. The words of grievers are powerful and their stories stirring, conveying how difficult it is to be in the world during this time of deep sorrow. Their passionate voices reflect their recognition that their lives are irrevocably changed.

VOICES OF GRIEF

Before my monthly pet loss support group, I think about who will be there. What will their stories be? How will they share their grief? For some, this may be a big step to come and uncover the wound of grief. There may be a strong fear of opening up and allowing themselves to feel the depth of what they are experiencing. Others may only want to sit and listen because to speak of the pain may be too hard. It simply hurts too much to tell the story. A few may fear it will trigger the depression they've fought all these years. For several, this will be the first time they've told their story. It may be the only time someone has asked to hear the story. Being in the group may allow a person to go to a level of grief not previously experienced. For some, this may be their second, third, or thirtieth time to attend our group. Others may come on an anniversary date, such as an animal's death or birthday.

One evening a woman made an observation as I put a box of tissues in the middle of the circle of chairs: "Some people sit around fires; we sit around a Kleenex box." Yes, traditionally, people have sat around fires and recounted stories that contained history, lessons, wisdom, and humor—which is worth remembering and passing on for safekeeping. We sit around our box of tissues and tell our stories. One person speaks, the rest of us listen. Speaking and listening from the heart are important steps to healing. The power of telling one's story with its potential for healing can be profound. At other times we laugh together as funny anecdotes are shared. Tears flow with both sad and humorous stories. There's a story behind each person and pet. Hearing these stories around the tissue box continues to remind me that these persons witness to the dominant place their animal companions had in their lives.

When I sit with people and they tell their stories, I not only hear the pain in their voices, but I also see their pain in their faces and bodies. They tell their stories with sadness and tears, anger and passion. Some are able to speak only in whispers. Others must stop speaking while they sob, for it's hard to talk when one's heart is breaking. Some can't find the words behind their grief, but their body says it all. I could put up a big banner on the wall that says, "Grief shared here." They relate the lessons and wisdom they learned from sharing their lives with their animals: lessons of mindfulness, living in the present, appreciating each moment, and experiencing the preciousness of a heartfelt connection. I find their stories compelling. Their stories show, beyond the shadow of a doubt, the bond of love they have shared with their cherished animals.

These people typically see that what they're experiencing is known to others. There's a felt connection. They no longer feel alone, but join with kindred others going through a similar experience. There's a sense of "You, too?" and "Me, too." The depth and intensity of grief is shared, legitimized, and validated.

INTENSITY AND DURATION OF GRIEF

After great love comes great grief. Mourners speak of being surprised by their grief in two important ways. The first is the overwhelming intensity and gut-wrenching nature of their grief; the second is its duration. They expected this time to be rough. They knew that the strength of their love would result in a depth of grief perhaps not experienced before. They couldn't imagine their lives without their animals. They anticipated being utterly bereft.

But just because they anticipated intellectually the heartbreaking loss doesn't make it hurt any less. People frequently express surprise at how strong their feelings are. They are astonished by the overwhelming sorrow, piercing grief, and emotional and spiritual trauma. They have never experienced that depth of loss before. The words they use reflect the intensity—"searing," "wrenching," "tormenting," and "ripping me apart." One woman said, "I learned the meaning of the word 'devastation.'" They simply did not expect to be so completely inconsolable. Rob noted:

I underrated the intensity of the loss I would feel in terms of the raw, emotional part, where the wave will come over you, and you just go completely to pieces for some time. There was more of that than I anticipated, feeling overwhelmed, hopeless and depressed. I thought I would feel those things, I just didn't anticipate they would have as much kick as they had.

Erica's voice also reflects this anguish:

At the beginning, it was awful; it was raw, stark, like a volcanic eruption. It was like nature's raw power unleashed. It was this primal and primitive kind of experience. I howled, I sobbed, I came home from the hospital and let it all out.

Patricia was fearful of the intensity of her feelings after her dog's death:

I would pray, "My God, just put me out of my misery," like I wanted God to do something to me. I wanted to fast forward to another time frame because I didn't know how to help myself. I said, "I don't know how to do this. I can't even put one foot in front of the other." I was at a loss for how I was going to get through it. Until now, I used to think I'm tough, I'm strong, I can basically handle anything. But Auggie's death knocked me for a loop, like somebody knocked my feet out from underneath me.

For some, the whole grief experience is frightening and unfamiliar. They have nothing in their past with which to relate these new intense feelings, nothing to reassure them and let them know they'll get through this time. Some people describe being nonfunctional and vegetative, thinking of their loss almost continuously in one way or another. Some disclose feeling suicidal. Others, while not actively suicidal, still question, "Why go on?"

Some mourners, such as Erica, understand the value of permitting themselves to feel the severity of their pain and despair:

> Whenever the grief would come up, I embraced all those feelings. I wouldn't try to suppress it. If I felt like I had to cry, I would let myself cry. I didn't try to fight it. It's ironic that by embracing the worst part of the pain, it made it easier to let go of it.

To feel these emotions can be formidable. One feels vulnerable. It can be scary to lament so intensely, especially for people who don't usually cry. It's disturbing to think that something's very wrong and one can't stop it. Similarly it's distressing to do things and feel emotions that one typically doesn't experience. Being reassured that these feelings and behaviors are common and natural responses to grief is important because bereaved pet guardians often think they are "sick," "crazy," or "losing it."

Robert said there were times when his grief overwhelmed him, and he clearly understood why. Basko was young, his death was unexpected, and he and Bonnie felt responsible. That combination had been overwhelming. He conceded there were times when he felt like, "Robert, you've got to get a grip here, because you're in danger of not getting your work done or not relating to people."

The depth of emotion one feels can also make others feel uncomfortable, awkward, and inadequate. That was Patricia's experience:

> It was hard for people who love me to see me miserable, unhappy, and sad. It was like, "Oh my God, what do we do? How do we fix this?" I said, "There isn't anything you can do, I'm just sad." A lot of people were not just concerned; they were really at odds as to how to deal with me.

Those grieving may engage in behaviors and make statements that seem alien to others' experience of grief. A person's experience of grief may be highly personal and unlike anyone else's. It can be difficult, if not impossible, for someone to go to the place of another's grief even when that person has experienced a similar grief. While there are similarities, there are also critical differences. Sharron believes that grief and its impact on a life is the most personal of emotions. "All people can really do is just be there with you; there is just nothing anyone can say or do."

At times atypical behaviors could be surprising. Erica found this to be true:

> I had this overwhelming compulsion to clean everything that belonged to him, as if symbolically I was cleansing away the cancer. It felt like a strange thing to do but it was so overwhelming. I also burnt sage at all those places in the apartment where he hung out. If he was going to some other plane of existence, I didn't want my greed to hold him back. Even in his death I was trying to take care of him and make sure the right thing happened.

Individuals described the cyclical nature of their grief as they spoke in terms of stages—at times wrenching and raw, at other times more muted—crescendos and diminuendos. Their grief passed through many metamorphoses. Erica said she never knew grief came in "so many infinite variations, sizes, shapes, and flavors." Additionally, pet parents were taken aback by the inconsistency of their reactions. Some days they'd be okay and other days they weren't. Erica summed up this experience:

> There are some days when I feel all the love I've ever felt for him and there's no little stinger of grief on the end of it. I just feel this love for him, and I have the feeling that wherever he is, he's okay. He's safe, and I think, "Wherever your path carries you, be safe, take care of yourself." I feel completely at peace and okay if I never see him again. But then, there are other days when it just rips me apart.

Not only were the grieving stunned by how deeply they were affected, they were also surprised they could hurt for so long. I talked with Debra eleven months after Addison's death. She still thought about him every day, though her pain was less. Then something would happen—a landmark day or event, for example, and she felt intense sadness again.

Debra told me about an unexpectedly difficult time when the veterinarian's assistant called to say Addison's ashes were ready. Previously, the only times they'd called her was when Addison was ready to come home after X rays, blood work, or a bath. Now they were calling to say he was "ready to be picked up." What did it mean to say he was "coming home"—how could he still be with her when he wasn't? She felt anxious and disquieted knowing his ashes were at the hospital. She couldn't leave him there, yet she didn't feel she could get them. She asked two friends to get and keep his ashes until she was emotionally able to take them.

Using figures of speech to describe one's grief is not unusual. "There's a hole in my heart" and "My heart is breaking" are common expressions. From time to time a metaphor of grief as waves is used. Once a woman described being on a beach where small ocean waves came up to her feet, ankles, or mid calves. Once in a while, a larger wave rolled in up to her knees and actually knocked her down, feeling like it could pull her under. She compared her grief for her animal to those ocean waves. She experienced continual small waves of grief coming in and going out, but occasionally a large wave of sorrow knocked her down and pulled her under. The large wave receded, however, and soon, she was back on her feet, steadied, experiencing again only the smaller waves.

There's no way to get around, over, or under the grief. To try to bulldoze oneself through it without the healing power of time is to abort healing.

DISBELIEF

Even if a death is expected or planned, when it comes, it's often shocking and surreal. Debra described how numb and dazed she felt after Addison's death as, "kind of cloudy, like in shock." She knew her friends helped her, brought her home, and sat with her, but, "I couldn't believe it was happening, that Addison wasn't here. . . ."

This stage provides time to absorb more gently the reality of the loss in increments one can handle. To assimilate the magnitude of the loss at once could be overwhelming. Being dazed gives one the time needed for a more gradual comprehension.

Numbness and disbelief can affect every area of a person's life. Ilana described what it was like to return to work:

> I felt like I was in another zone for about a week. I felt like I had landed on another planet and almost didn't feel capable of going to work because I didn't feel like I could concentrate.

This is a period to be gentle with oneself—to take care of oneself in loving and comforting ways, and to accept others' nurturing.

ANGER

Anger can range from annoyance to outrage. It can be experienced emotionally, physically, cognitively, behaviorally, and spiritually. The anger can be directed at a number of people.

First, anger is felt toward family, friends, or co-workers who don't understand why someone would grieve so deeply for an animal. Anger arises because the type and level of support and understanding needed is unavailable. One's experience of loss is negated when others say, "It was just a cat, for heaven's sake" or "So, when are you going to get another one?" The degree of hurt and anger that comes from uncaring or misguided statements results in feeling misunderstood and invalidated. Such tactlessness and insensitivity have damaged or ended relationships.

Next, anger can be directed toward a friend, family member, or hired service provider who was responsible for the care of the animal. This person's recklessness may have caused an animal's death by accident, injury, or disease.

Third, anger can be felt toward the veterinary staff because of a perception of negligent or incompetent care. People who feel their pets have been inexcusably misdiagnosed are bitter that valuable time marched on as their animals were inappropriately treated. Veterinary mismanagement is felt to have hastened the decline and contributed to a nightmarish illness. When an animal goes to the best vets, sees specialists, has major and extensive diagnostic procedures, and something is missed by simple oversight, the owner feels not only anger toward, but also betrayal by, the veterinary staff. Individuals seek ways to dispel the intensity of their anger. Some confront the veterinarian. A few want to contact the state veterinary licensing board. Others want to take legal action. Alternatively, sometimes anger isn't due to perceived veterinary incompetence as much as simply questions as to whether something additional or different might have been done in terms of treatment decisions.

Anger can be felt toward those who had a role in the animal's death by acts of omission or commission. Take, for instance, the driver who hits an animal or the owner whose pet is attacked and killed by an aggressive dog that was off its leash. Where possible, people may consider seeking legal recourse.

Anger can also be directed toward God for letting such a thing happen to a beloved pet. For someone who believed in God's goodness, to experience a situation that seems to negate that perceived benevolence is to experience a sense of betrayal, disappointment, and anger. One woman lost all faith in God after the accidental death of her dog, "How could God take away the one source of light in my life?"

Further, anger can be felt toward other animals in the home. The remaining animals aren't as loving, affectionate, cuddly, supportive, or nurturing. They aren't the favorite. They may, in fact, be perceived as having contributed to the deceased pet's death by having been a major source of stress.

One woman described her feelings of resentment when she saw cats that could eat. Because her cat couldn't eat after the first two weeks of his illness, anytime she saw a television cat food commercial, she'd get angry at the unfairness, "How dare those cats be healthy and able to eat when my wonderful little guy wasted away and died."

Moreover, anger can be felt toward the faceless others who go about their lives as if nothing has happened. It's as if two separate worlds are occurring simultaneously. There's the world where people are drinking their coffee, attending their social functions, and going to work as if nothing is different. In stark contrast, there's the world of the grieving pet parent, the world that has been turned upside down. Anger is felt toward all those who simply have no idea what has happened.

Finally, anger can be directed toward self—for feeling "stupid," "insensitive," "careless," and "unworthy of the pet." When people feel responsible for the death of an animal, or feel they didn't manage the care correctly, self-reproach and self-hatred can tear those individuals apart. For instance, one woman repeatedly berated herself, saying she deserved to suffer because of how she had accidentally backed over her dog in the driveway.

GUILT

Guilt was all-pervasive in a recent group. As individuals told their stories, each person, without exception, voiced guilt:

"I feel so guilty that I couldn't afford the additional $1,000 that more tests would have required."

"I held him in my arms as he was put to sleep, and I was wracked with guilt."

"I feel so guilty that I wasn't with her when she died because I was out of town."

"I feel so guilty for what I had to do—when I was depressed, he saved my life, and I couldn't do that for him."

"I feel so guilty that I couldn't find an apartment that would take pets so I could get him up here before he died."

"I feel guilty because I didn't get to say good-bye."

"Her euthanasia wasn't gentle; it was an awful ending, and I feel guilty about that. That's not how I had planned it or how I wanted it to be."

"We struggled with the decision for months, and even though I know it was the right thing for her, I still feel so guilty because I was playing God, and I didn't want to do that."

Month after month I hear similar expressions of guilt. Guilt seems to be part of the contextual fabric surrounding an animal's death. Guilt consumes people because of their remorse and self-blame for perceived acts of commission or omission. Self-blame for "not doing well enough" with decisions made; self-criticism for "not doing good enough" with care given; an inability to forgive oneself for not measuring up to a perceived standard in one's mind—each of these dimensions can be part of the experience of guilt.

Robert's story revealed the torment of guilt he and Bonnie felt over Basko's death:

We feel responsible. We are responsible that we took him into harm's way and are the reason he died. I feel really stupid about the whole thing. I just didn't think—it was too hot, the altitude was too high, it just wasn't the right thing to do. I should have been more cognizant of the situation. Those things are really weighing on us.

A critical point at which guilt is commonly experienced is euthanasia. Accompanying that weighty and consequential decision can be the horrendous sense of playing God and the outright abhorrence of that responsibility. Moreover, another source of guilt is the timeliness at which euthanasia occurs—"I should have done it sooner; I hate it that she suffered those last few days" or "I should have waited a little bit longer; maybe he would have gotten better if I'd just tried a little longer." Whatever decisions were made, people often feel they weren't the right ones, and now they blame themselves. There's a sense of, "If only I could turn back the clock."

Guilt can be as pervasive as grief, the two being closely intertwined. Guilt can be toxic and exacerbate grief. As one feels more guilt over the death, grief intensifies and worsens. Guilt can result in utterly wrenching emotional pain. Recently a woman said every time she experiences her guilt, it feels like she's ripping open a wound.

In the face of all the guilt experienced, I have the following bedrock belief: it's truly the exception that people did not act as best they could for their animals' highest good. They acted on their animals' behalf with the goal of having the best possible outcome and quality of life. Whatever decisions or choices were made, they were based on love and a consideration for the animal.

Now, looking back, people would have made other choices. Accidents happen. I learned that. With hindsight, a different action now would be selected. But the fact that a particular choice was made or action was taken does not negate pet parents' love and devotion for their animals. One did not knowingly or deliberately cause harm. After twenty years, this belief is a major unequivocal component of my truth.

Please Don't Feel Guilty

Please don't feel guilty. You don't need to. I don't want you to be rough on yourself. I heard you speak last night. I heard you say how guilty you are for what you think you didn't do right. You did more than I ever would have expected anyone to do. You loved me through it all. I never doubted your love for me. Whatever decisions you made, I know were made with my best interest in mind. Please don't feel guilty. It breaks my heart to hear you speak of your guilt. You don't need to feel guilty. Please don't.
        —Betty J. Carmack

GRIEF THAT IS PHYSICAL

Mourners relate stories of grief as a visceral experience with physical manifestations. Crying, sobbing, nightmares, sleeplessness, and loss of appetite are exhausting. People feel ill and weak: "I'm sick to my stomach," "I just want to throw up," and "It just makes you sick." Their descriptions reflect their bodies trying to process the pain that packs a real wallop. An aching in their stomach or their heart captures the piercing and raw pain: "It just hurts," "I don't think my heart will survive this," and "It just feels like a knife in there." It's also common to have tightness in the chest, making it hard to breathe. Jyl described feeling a huge chasm between her head and her feet, as if a part of her had disappeared, as if her heart had been removed.

Using the analogy of an artesian well of grief inside her, Erica said, "Pure grief bubbles up from the core of my being, and it hurts in a physical way that he's not here. It's this palpable thing that I can touch, pure grief."

Some experience their physical grief only during waking hours while others also live it through dreams. Some dreams are disturbing, renewing feelings of running against time and not being able to save one's animal. Patricia felt this way:

> I kept having a recurring nightmare of the whole thing that happened. It would startle me awake. It was freaking me out. I'd think, "Enough already, it's the third month already." This was not only disruptive, it was causing me physical repercussions. I'm not eating, I'm not sleeping, I'm not this, I'm not that. It was close to debilitating because I felt so out of whack.

CONTINUED SENSE OF PRESENCE

Time after time I hear stories of people who have seen, heard, and felt their animals after their deaths. Many find comfort in the idea that their animal's spirit might still be present. Out of the corner of their eye they've seen what appears to be a glimpse or shadow of their pet. They've heard tags on a collar, or their animal's breathing or footsteps. They've felt their companion's presence on their bed or felt its weight walking around. They've experienced the actual presence and energy of their companion animal. One woman recently described how she felt the same physical warmth of her dog's body against her chest as she had when she'd held him in this position when he was living.

Elizabeth described how she put the box of ashes of her cat, Smokey, on the steps. She told him he was home and that he could "run on upstairs." "I saw a grayness running by me and felt this was Smokey's presence coming back home." Before his death, whenever she'd brought him into the house, she'd tell him, "Run on upstairs now, you're home."

Others are convinced, too, that what they hear, see, smell and feel is their animal's spirit. Janet says of Missy, "I still feel she's with us. Many days I have a sense of her and have to check to be sure she isn't right around the corner. She's always with me."

One night Don was awakened by what sounded like a pet's tag knocking against a dish. He first thought it was his cat, Scooter. Yet, when he sat up in bed, Scooter was actually on the bed, also awake and listening. The next morning Tony, Don's partner, commented to Don about the sound he'd heard during the night of a tag hitting a dish. Their beloved sixteen-year-old cat, Monkey, had passed two weeks earlier, and they each believe that the sound they heard was Monkey's spirit coming back to visit. For each of them this was comforting.

On the night her cat died, Rosemary felt his presence on her pillow and heard his purring. She was unsure if this was real, a dream, or her imagination, but she felt him beside her. She believed this was his way of telling her that he was alright.

ABSENCE OF PRESENCE

After great presence comes great absence. The animal's absence is prevalent and widespread. Paradoxically, the silence accompanying the absence is unbearably loud. When the physical and spiritual presence has been so pervasive, its absence brings devastation, desolation, emptiness, and quietness. Rob described this experience following Zomax's death:

> It's disorienting to wake up without her and go to sleep without her. We lived in such close quarters. When we were awake, she wanted to be in the same room I was in. That physical presence, the sounds and smell of another living being—in its absence, there's a loud noise. I still sometimes expect to see her when I go around the corner.

All the daily routines and ritualized interactions with one's animal companion are no more. Little things become huge reminders. Pets aren't there to nuzzle and burrow under the covers. One woman gained five pounds following her cat's death because she used to sit and hold him while they'd watch TV. Afterwards she sat and ate. One of the hardest times is coming home, opening the door, and realizing the animal is not there. Some people say they're caught off guard because on some level they still expect their animal to greet them. Feelings of disorientation and being caught by surprise mark the absence. Time and again these grievers say, "I still catch myself, even after all this time." Rob described these moments of being caught off guard as the hardest. "It's the pet equivalent of catching oneself setting a place at the table for someone who's gone." In contrast, knowing that a particular event might be difficult can help people prepare themselves and position their defenses.

Physical items—food and water bowls, blankets, scratching posts, cages, kitty condos, leashes and collars with tags, food, bedding, medicines, litter boxes, and toys—all serve as painful reminders that a beloved animal is not physically present anymore. Some people put these items away immediately because they are too painful to see. They don't want these reminders that their pet is no longer present. They vacuum to remove all traces of fur or hair. They get rid of all physical evidence and put the photographs away.

Others receive comfort from these tangible objects and actually feel closer to their animal when these remembrances are visible. They like finding whiskers, nails or little clumps of fur or hair. They keep treasure boxes with whiskers, nails, baby teeth, fur, collars, and tags. Some describe the solace they feel when they wrap themselves in an animal's blanket or bedding. Some wear their animal's tags on a chain around their neck. One woman wore her dog's collar for the first few days after the death. Another wears a heart shaped locket with a bit of her dog's hair inside. All do this to feel closer to their animal companion.

Some choose to leave things as they were when the animal last used them—the ball in the back yard, the toy on the floor, the rumpled bedding, the litter box with the cat's scratchings. Some give the food and medicines to an animal organization. Others hold on to keepsakes as a way to feel connected. Some find comfort in thinking that future animal companions will use a treasured bowl, leash, or collar. Their pet will live on as another animal eventually enjoys the items. For other persons, this is counter to their inclinations.

Still others describe it as a "mixed bag." In some respect, items are comforting, and in others they're too painful a reminder. They do what they call "flip-flopping." Some put mementos away for awhile, pulling them back out later. Others put particular objects away while keeping others accessible. One woman still has her dog's medications after seventeen years. She'd never consider using them for her current pets, but because they are her last tangible connection to her dog, she isn't ready to let them go.

It's not unusual for family members to have differing viewpoints. Jody felt that Kasha's belongings, like her food and brushes, didn't need to be in "Kasha's drawer" any longer. Rachel, Kasha's other mom, had a different perspective: she felt it was still Kasha's space, and she wasn't yet ready for it not to be.

LIFE IS DIFFERENT

Unequivocally, life has changed. Some feel this is the end of a chapter, others the end of a book. Still others feel it's more like the end of their world as they knew it. For many the idea of "getting back to normal" is impossible. Others describe their "world becoming silent" or "time stopping." However perceived, losing a beloved animal companion is a life-altering experience. Patricia found this to be true:

> I read a book in which a woman described her life as black and white since her pet passed away, and I thought, "Exactly. Life's still going on all around me. Everybody's in place. But it's like things now are in black and white."

Erica compared her grief experience to that period following the 1989 earthquake in the San Francisco Bay Area. A considerable part of people's lives and routines returned to normal, at least in some ways. But some things were irrevocably changed. Similarly after her cat's death, while some aspects of her life were returning to normal, others were "never ever" going to be the same:

> I'm not the same person I was three months ago. There's a real sadness in my life. On one hand I'm richer for having had him in my life, but I feel less now that he's not here. I feel there's a big chunk of my life that's gone.

Ilana concurred that life was incongruous:

> I walked around traumatized. We'd go into a coffee store on the way to the hospital to visit the animals and people around us were normal and happy. The sun was shining and "How are you doing?" and "Have a nice day"—that usual American approach. I couldn't think of anything positive. I was so devastated. How could this have happened to our animals?

Ilana felt she and her life had been unmistakably changed by the fire and its attendant multiple losses. "One moment your life is normal, and the next everything is totally upside down. I don't think I'll ever see or hear a fire truck again without intensely personalizing it and reliving some of that emotion." Her previous sense of security was now gone. She no longer felt safe leaving her animals at home.

When I came home after my rafting accident and the loss of Rocky, my house was painfully empty. There was no life energy at all; the place felt dead. Before, his energy and presence had been so strong. "Before" was no more. I wandered from room to room, seeking him, even though, intellectually, I knew he wasn't there. It was a yearning, a searching, and a longing, like I was a child, lost without my source of security and comfort. Time crawled by. I tried to sleep, but I slept poorly. My life felt so unbelievably alien, and the changes had occurred within minutes. There was no time to get ready.

Another way in which life is different is the realization that one's identity as "pet mom" or "pet dad" is gone. Feeling stripped of the pet parent identity, people no longer feel they belong in that group. Some avoid pet related commercials, stores, departments, events, and other references to companion animals. On the other hand, others crave and seek out the pleasure of further animal companionship through family's, friends' or neighbors' animals.

Patricia had Auggie for almost thirteen years, a third of Patricia's life. After his death Patricia didn't go down the dog food aisle in the store. She didn't dare look at anything pet-oriented because she didn't feel she had that privilege anymore. She'd like "to travel down the pet food aisle" again, but after Auggie's death, it was too painful, "All of a sudden, just *boom!* You don't realize how much a part of your daily life and interaction that was."

I wonder if some losses are ever completely resolved. The body, mind, emotions, and spirit remember. Certainly the time required to resolve a painful loss is infinitely longer than society provides us. Ilana said it had been more than one and a half years and she hadn't resolved her grief. For another woman it's been three years, and she recently came back to the group. It was the anniversary of her cat's death, and there were still some issues she wanted to discuss. Another time a woman said when she went back to reread and reflect on a series of animal losses she had experienced years earlier, she felt the same intensity of emotions she originally had. For me, too, as I've written this book and remembered the deaths of Rocky, Puccini, and Sunshine, my eyes have welled with tears as I've recalled and relived particular moments.

Some people recollect every detail of an animal's death. It's as if the memories are seared into their minds. Betty, age thirty-six, vividly remembers the death of her dog, Candy, that occurred twenty years ago:

> I remember everything about that day. I remember lying in bed hearing my parents talk about it downstairs. I pretended to be asleep so I wouldn't have to face it. I remember everything. I couldn't stay in the room when they did it. My mother stayed with her. I waited, sobbing, in the car. That is my one regret, that I didn't stay with her. I feel like I abandoned her when she needed me.

NOT NEEDED ANYMORE

After their animals' deaths, some people say they feel as if they're not needed. They don't know what to do with themselves and feel at loose ends. This is especially true when an animal needed 'round-the-clock care or consumed one's consciousness twenty-four hours a day, seven days a week. Erica summed up this experience:

> I sat around the house for a couple of days, thinking, I don't like this. Nothing to do, nobody to take care of, nobody who needs me, nobody I can comfort, nobody to come and comfort me. It was really tough and very uncomfortable, almost more uncomfortable than taking care of Mao while he was dying.

OTHER ANIMAL COMPANIONS' GRIEF

Connections between animals are quite strong. Stories are told of how remaining animals grieve for the one that's gone. They appear unsettled, quieter, and depressed with disrupted routines. They seem perplexed, searching for the missing animal. The remaining one may have been a litter mate, mother, father, son, or daughter of the deceased. For some individuals their remaining pets' grief is an additional concern requiring extra care and love.

When Sophia, a Brittany spaniel puppy, was brought into Paule and Gina's home, Pasta, their cat, was so angry he spent the entire first year in the basement. Much later Pasta and Sophia actually became quite close and when the two would be separated for short periods of time, Sophia would lick Pasta when they were reunited. Additionally, Pasta served as Sophia's pillow when they'd lie together on the couch.

After Sophia's death, Paule and Gina kept Sophia's body in the basement to enable Pasta to be with her and know she had died. Paule said it broke Pasta's heart to lose his sister of seventeen years. For weeks Pasta slept on Sophia's cushions even though he had never slept on them while Sophia was living. For the first week Pasta didn't eat. Following that week, he got up to eat and use the litter box but went back immediately to Sophia's cushions where he stayed. After a few weeks and the cushions had become quite dirty, Paule washed them. Afterwards, Pasta never went back to the cushions. Within three months, Pasta, nineteen years old, became ill and died. Paule believes the loss of Sophia hastened his death.

Sensitivity to remaining pets is also reflected in the story Michelle and Paul told. When their Airedale, Sam, was to be euthanized, their veterinarian asked them to bring Tasha, Sam's younger sister. Because Tasha had been utterly dependent on Sam for her sense of security, the doctor anticipated that Tasha would have a difficult time with Sam's death. Additionally, she thought if Tasha were present for the euthanasia, she wouldn't be looking for Sam, but instead, would know that Sam had died. At the hospital, after the veterinarian gave Sam an injection to relax him, Michelle and Paul remained on the floor with him. In a highly unusual manner, Tasha never went over to Sam. Typically, the two were all over each other, but today was different. After Sam's death, the doctor called Tasha over to Sam, but Tasha refused to go.

Persons are encouraged to keep something of the deceased animal around so remaining animals can smell it. Michelle and Paul kept Sam's bed, and Tasha would lay on it. Tasha continued this for about a month but then stopped. Michelle and Paul felt that Tasha had a difficult time with Sam's death. She wasn't as perky or happy as she usually was. She wasn't responsive to invitations to go for walks. Increasingly, she wanted to be around Michelle and Paul, who felt they couldn't leave her alone because of her insecurity and fear.

On the other hand, other individuals don't see a discernable grieving response in their remaining animals. These animals hardly seem to notice that anything is different and many times actually enjoy the increased attention and new status they now have.

COPING/RESOURCES

Moving through grief requires a variety of coping resources. Spiritual resources are powerful in the way they illuminate the darkness of sorrow and despair. Sharron acknowledged that a driving force for her was her search for a deeper spirituality. Her quest began when Stan, her partner, died a few years earlier. She credits her deepened spirituality as being one key to her survival after her dog's death. Trying to frame this latest loss within a spiritual context, she sought the lessons surrounding Gigi's life and death.

Erica, too, recognized her spirituality as an anchor, "I think my spiritual beliefs that I practiced long before Mao got sick helped me get through the experience. Just the fact that I know our spirits live on helped me."

Ilana initially managed by being caregiver and protector. When her dogs came home from the hospital, they needed 'round-the-clock care—eye medications, antibiotic administration, foot soaks to burned feet, and steam treatments to aid breathing. Serving in the caregiver role gave Ilana a sense of purpose. Being strong and in charge empowered her to feel less helpless.

Patricia described what helped her cope:

> What got me through the past three months was trying to get from one day to the next, one hour to the next, one week to the next. It helped to have other things on the agenda, to be able to work on Auggie's scrapbook and garden. It helped being involved and active, trying to do things to make it more purposeful, rather than just sitting and being sad.

Furthermore, Patricia didn't pretend things were better than they were:

> What helped me most was letting people know this wasn't something I was going to bounce back from. "I'm very sad and depressed; I can't make small talk. I can't talk on the phone. I just can't." What helped me was I didn't try to do that. This wasn't a temporary state of affairs. I was devastated.

Some attended church more. Many read self-help books about grief, loss in general, and pet loss specifically. Some saw counselors and therapists. Others attended pet loss groups. Debra told her new dog, Chloe, about Addison and their life together. Jyl described the comfort she felt from the cuddliness and soulfulness in the expressions of her dog "Beanie Babies" toys.

Sharron said, "You just go on. I can't undo this, as much as I'd like to. I just try and keep going forward, that's all I can do." When Gigi died, the life she'd known no longer existed. Now she was trying to build a new life for herself. She credited her ability to move forward with "just doing it, from sheer determination."

A few chose to consult psychics. For Patricia, the consultation was a major turning point:

> After talking with her, I realized I couldn't have done anything differently. Auggie knew I did everything within my power. Now I feel he doesn't have an ax to grind with me. I have to accept that. I feel calmer and more reassured that he's at peace. I still cry, but it's not a cry of remorse. It's more of a loneliness and missing.

Elinor felt that in her ignorance, she had betrayed Idgie's trust, but she didn't think he would agree with that. As a result she tried to remember his death from his perspective. Keeping that perspective helped Elinor cope by understanding that Idgie wouldn't expect the same things she expected of herself.

Many people draw on practical and emotional support offered by friends and family to help sustain them. Erica found such support helpful:

> When I started telling my friends what happened, I got so much support from them. It felt like a little buffer zone between me and the worst part of my grief. I felt insulated, like I was in this little safe space.

Friends and family who can be present in the midst of sadness and darkness are true gifts to their healing process. People who are supportive and don't disregard the grievers' feelings make a significant difference. What they're feeling is too tender and precious to be trampled. Grieving pet parents long to be nurtured, not invalidated. Those whose lives and hearts are touched by an outpouring of love and understanding feel truly blessed.

For some, to grieve with remaining family animals is comforting. There's a tenderness and closeness as they share a loss together. When other animals need their love and attention, it lets them feel needed. For others, these remaining pets only intensify their grief and feel more like a burden.

People are often surprised by the quality of their coping strategies. Some who thought they had sufficient resources find that the depth and extent of this painful loss severely challenges their resources. Others are gratefully surprised by the depth and extent of what they are able to draw upon.

DIFFERENCES/SIMILARITIES TO OTHER GRIEF

Repeatedly I hear, "I grieved more for my animal than I ever did for my parent"—or sibling, child, spouse, or partner. I'm continually struck by both the similarities and dissimilarities between the grief for an animal companion and the grief for a person. The depth, intensity, and length might be the same, or, depending on the relationship, different.

Rachel compared her grief for her sister with that for her dog, Kasha:

> My sister and I had almost fifty years of shared history. Kasha and I had thirteen. But it was different because I lived with Kasha every day, except for vacations. Emotionally, it was similar. Grief is grief. The grief itself hasn't been all that different. I'm still going through it, it's still painful. I'm crying now about Kasha. Sometimes I still cry for my sister, too. It really isn't that different.

Our grief for our animal companions can be more acute and intense and last longer than the grief we feel when a human dies. Our lives with our animals are typically closer than our lives with humans. Relationships with humans are fraught with ambivalence and conflict, whereas relationships with pets are more pure, uncluttered, unspoiled, and based on unconditional love and trust. Jody described how the nature of her relationship with her dog affected her grief:

> Because she was such a part of my life, my grief is much more intense. Kasha was in our lives every single day, she was ours.

She was part of our life. She was like our child. We brought her up, she grew up with us. We raised her. We took care of her health needs. We talk about Kasha all the time, and we probably will forever. Kasha's everlasting to me.

The degree and extent of support available is usually less for a pet's death than for the death of a person. While there is increased understanding about grief accompanying pet loss, there are still those who say, "It was just an animal" or "Why is she so upset? It was just a bird. Get another one." The way in which the world often minimizes the loss accentuates the feelings of grief. One doesn't get bereavement leave when an animal companion dies. Workplaces don't usually respond with any recognition of the death. Coworkers are uncertain how to behave so they often do nothing, leaving a person feeling as if no one really cares. After human death, there are cards, visits, wakes, funerals, flowers, gifts of food, and memorial donations. Such responses aren't typical when a pet dies. One's reality is frequently negated by the minimization of others. Though others may think, "It's no big deal," to the griever it *is* a big deal, and it matters profoundly. Frequently, because grieving persons anticipate negative reactions, they choose not to disclose their loss, increasing their sense of isolation and lack of support.

CONTEXTUAL FACTORS

Sometimes the grief experienced for an animal companion is compounded by a person's other losses. The loss of an animal can come at the time a relationship is ending through divorce or separation. One may lose a partner, spouse, home, and an animal, which creates multiple losses on varied levels. Or the animal may have been a major connection to a significant other. Significant others can be those who have already passed on, such as a spouse, friend, sibling, partner, child, parent or pet, or those who are still living.

Other contextual factors can contribute to one's grief. From time to time a pet's health status parallels that of a pet parent. Or the similarity of a pet's death to the death of a significant other can reignite the earlier grief and make the present grief even more difficult. When Nicholas, Sally's beloved cat, died suddenly and unexpectedly from a probable cardiac condition, his death triggered a return of the deep grief and sadness she had experienced when her mother died in a similar way from a similar condition. Now Sally was grieving not only for Nicholas, but also again for her mother, whom she loved deeply. People have described their animal's death as "eerily similar" to that of a significant other's years earlier.

Gigi was adopted by Sharron and Stan after Sharron's sister, Judy, died. As a result, Gigi was a strong connection to both Judy and Stan. Sharron knew Gigi's death would be horrible because of her love for Gigi. But because Stan died before Gigi did, Sharron also felt she lost her last attachment to Stan and Judy when Gigi died.

Ilana described a particularly disturbing circumstance. She'd left the veterinary hospital at 4:00 A.M., and by late morning, people were showing her a front page newspaper article with photographs, detailing her apartment fire. She was angry that this article was on the front page, capitalizing on their catastrophe, "It's not just a fire or a disaster; it's our story. That's our cat and to show his suffering on the front page felt like ambulance chasing."

Elinor disclosed the multiple horrific pet losses she experienced in childhood as a result of her parents' and brother's violence, torture, and neglect of family pets. Her family, who considered animals disposable, were profoundly abusive and disrespectful of life. In contrast, Elinor bonded to, and found substantial comfort in the kindness, gentleness, and love of the animals. Her animals were her true family, and she received from them what she didn't get from her human family.

As a child who loved animals, she fought valiantly for these family pets, but her feelings, wishes, and efforts were continuously denied and overruled. The emotional trauma she experienced in seeing her animals abused and killed was inexcusable and cruel. She recounted the tragic and horrifying circumstances of each pet's death, and the powerlessness she felt as a child in stopping these sadistic abuses. Elinor says she still dreams of, and grieves for, her animals who died thirty to forty years ago.

Now as an adult, she freely opens her home to cats and gives them ongoing love and devotion. She cares deeply for her animal family. Their shared lives are filled with joy and reciprocal nurturance. Yet, as Elinor grieved the death of Idgie, her mother's harsh, screaming criticism for Elinor's "stupidity" in relation to a childhood pet's death echoed in her mind. Elinor chastised herself for what she felt was her role in Idgie's death.

The intensity of grief can also be felt at an anniversary of a death. People are often caught off guard by the strength of their grief as the anniversary date approaches. They characterize it as an intensity, "like a crescendo," leading up to the marker of the death.

I, too, was stunned by my response to the first anniversary of Rocky's death. For several weeks I was cognizant of the approaching date, but had no particularly strong physical or emotional responses. However, a day or two before the actual date as I thought of the way he died, I experienced increased anxiety, both viscerally and emotionally. My stomach felt it, and my mind felt it. I felt vulnerable and frightened, and many of the powerful initial feelings of grief resurfaced. Because these feelings were so disturbing, I tried to push them away. On the actual anniversary day, however, I could not suppress them. As late morning approached, a darkening wave of emotion began to engulf me. My world became increasingly overcast. A shadow began to cover my world, mind, spirit, and body. I felt as if I was having my own personal eclipse. It began about 11:30 A.M. As it got closer to 1:40 P.M., the shadow was more complete, until I felt I was in total eclipse, covered in an oppressive darkness. At that time, I was lying on the sofa in my living room, experiencing profound sadness and actual physical symptoms of grief. All my bodily processes felt slowed, as if in a deep depression. At the core of my being, I reexperienced losing Rocky the year before.

It wasn't long before my "eclipse" began to recede. I felt my own light, life, and energy returning. Within an hour, I was out of the shadow and darkness. I had, though, at the center of my being, reexperienced a very real and strong visceral, emotional, and spiritual response to Rocky's loss. As with so many other aspects of his death, I learned again, with humility, that theories about grief and bereavement also applied to me. I wasn't immune.

On subsequent anniversary dates my response was never as strong. On the first anniversaries for both Puccini and Sunshine, I noted the date, felt some grief and sadness and remembered each with tenderness and love, recalling their endearing places in my life. But that primal response for Rocky was never duplicated in my responses to their anniversaries. I believe it had to do with the difference in the nature and circumstances of the deaths.

CHILDREN'S GRIEF
The grief that some children feel can be like that of adults— intense, unfamiliar, threatening, and frightening. For many children, their pets are their best friends and confidants. Their feelings of anger, sorrow, and self-blame are just as real as those of adults.

Six-year-old Allie and I went to lunch so she could tell me about her Palomino pony, Paul, who died last year of a heart attack. Allie started riding Paul when she was four years old. Allie said Paul, who was scared of most things, became frightened by something happening in the next stall, "spooked," fell, and died.

Allie said she "really loved Paul," and she hurt inside when he died. "I cried and cried for weeks. It's hard. You try your best not to think about it. Your parents try to soothe you, but it doesn't make it any better. You just try to live through it by yourself."

Her dog, Chewie, helped her. She said Chewie knew she was unhappy, and when he barked, he was talking about it because he'd been at the ranch and knew what happened. Drawing pictures of Paul also helped her, but she didn't want to be with the other horses or riders because the memories were too painful. She didn't want anyone talking about Paul, including her mother and father. The only person she wanted to talk to was her friend, Stevie, because each knew how the other felt.

Allie now has another horse, Secret. Even though she says that she's "now over it" her little voice clearly and convincingly described the real and intense grief that children like Allie experience.

While Allie's loss was sudden and unexpected, Stephanie's was gradual and anticipated. Stephanie, nine years old, told me her story about the death of her golden hamster, Fluffy, who died last year. During the two and a half years that Stephanie had Fluffy, she had responsibility for his care, "He was my friend, he gave me love, and I felt safe with him," she said. "He was a nice little pet, he was sweet. He was just my pet, my favorite pet." Fluffy died from a tumor on his back leg. He gradually became slower and slower and eventually couldn't walk to his food dish. As she held him in a towel the day before he died, Stephanie was aware that his death was fast approaching. She described how sad she felt and acknowledged how much she loved him. When he actually died, Stephanie felt even more grief because of "all those years I had him and loved him." Her good friend, Georgia, was at her house at the time of Fluffy's death. "She encouraged me, she told me it's okay, and that everyone has to come to that point at some time." Stephanie acknowledged being thankful that Fluffy was now out of his pain, but her thankfulness was mixed with sorrow that they wouldn't be together to play anymore.

Later Stephanie and her family, in addition to some of her friends, had a funeral for Fluffy. They placed Fluffy in a box with tissue, and Stephanie made a wooden cross on which she wrote his name. At the service Stephanie and others spoke lovingly of Fluffy. They buried him and placed the cross at his gravesite.

Stephanie told me that the support she received from her mother and her friend was most helpful as she grieved. Stephanie felt supported when her mother understood her grief, said comforting things, and gave her hugs.

When I asked her what she would tell other boys and girls whose animal companions die, she answered, "If a pet dies and is in pain, its death is a good thing because the pet isn't in any more pain. It's also something that will happen to everyone, it's part of the circle of life. Encourage the children that it will be okay. Hug them, and show them you understand." Stephanie ended our conversation by saying she knew she did the best she could for Fluffy, and in her heart she knew she'd loved him well.

Some adults who attend pet loss support groups speak not only of their current grief but also of the grief they experienced as children when their pets died. They express their anger and hurt, and describe their sense of betrayal if there was parental dishonesty about an animal's death. Worse, they hurt now because they weren't helped to grieve for their cherished animal then.

Based on Allie's and Stephanie's stories, and those of many others who have shared childhood memories, I offer the following guidelines for those helping children in grief: Be honest as you give them information and answer their questions. Talk with them at their level of development, using simple language for younger children, and more advanced explanations for more mature and older youth. Respect and honor their feelings. Include them in rituals to honor their beloved animal's memory. Offer them ways to express their grief through play, art, music, dance, stories, and drama. Offer them choices of what aspects of the animal's care, dying, and after-death rituals they want to share.

ELDERS' GRIEF

Just as pet loss affects children in profound ways, so, too, does it affect the elderly. In the first chapter we explored some of the ways animal companions impact our lives as family members, sustainers through difficult times, and sources of reciprocal nurturance. Consider the increased relevance of these benefits for an elderly individual. Think about the large number of role transitions, losses, and changes that occur in the lives of the elderly. Reflect on how profoundly important it is for an elderly person to experience the physical and psychological advantages that a pet gives. For those elderly who are homebound or whose world has become increasingly limited, their animals often provide their only source of affection, love, companionship, nurture, structure, and predictability in their lives.

Such a loss is huge. For some elderly persons, their animal companions are their only family. Additionally, the pet who dies may be one final link to a former spouse, partner, friend, child, sibling, or home and, thus, the grief is intensified. A woman who attended my group fifteen years ago clearly conveyed that her cats were closer and more important to her than her human family had ever been. She was utterly bereft and inconsolable when her two cats—her family—died within weeks of each other. Once an animal dies, the elderly are frequently hesitant to get another because of their realistic fear that the new animal will outlive them. They worry about the uncertain aftermath for the animal after they, the caregivers, die.

LOSS OF AN ASSISTANCE ANIMAL

Assistance animals help those challenged by vision, hearing, mobility, and social limitations. Like pets, these animals provide companionship, but they also provide much more. They represent independence and the ability to function more fully in the world. They symbolize sight, hearing, mobility, and socialization.

The loss of an assistance animal presents a unique type of loss. Sometimes an assistance animal becomes ill and dies suddenly and unexpectedly. Other times assistance animals develop chronic illnesses that leave them unable to work. Yet, even without illness, an assistance animal is usually retired after approximately seven years of service.

When a person has to give up an assistance animal and begin to work with another, a whole gamut of emotions is experienced: loss, sadness, vulnerability, and separation, as well as optimism and hope. The deck has been reshuffled. I remember a conversation I had ten years ago with a group of individuals who had assistance animals. They told me of their inability to grieve fully the loss of a former animal because of their need to begin immediate work with a new animal. Having lost the ability to see, hear, walk, or stand up, these individuals must immediately bond with another assistance animal. The quality of their life depends on their ability to develop a working relationship with a new animal, and there simply isn't the time or opportunity to grieve as they'd like. The new relationship takes front stage as the grieving, by necessity, takes back stage.

. . . a time to weep, a time to mourn . . .

Chapter 5

A Time to Heal

"a time to heal . . . a time for peace"
(Eccles. 3:3, 8)

Out of all this pain, I got more insight, and I became a stronger person. After Mao died, when I realized what kind of experience I had, I felt more whole and integrated as a person.
—*Erica*

In the depths of sadness, pain, and despair, it's hard to imagine that one will ever feel good again. Grieving pet parents struggle through the darkness of this consequential and momentous loss. Their lives feel irrevocably changed. It's sometimes impossible to think that they can ever get through it, much less over it. Can light illuminate the darkness? Unreal. Can they remember and move on? Unthinkable. Could they possibly heal? Unimaginable. Could this be a place of transformation? Incomprehensible. Memories can hurt.

I, too, remember feeling that way when Rocky died. I had nothing to relate to that gave me any assurance that I would get through this, my first major loss. I felt I'd never enjoy anything again. I couldn't believe I'd ever feel like I wasn't just going through the motions. I thought I'd never feel whole again.

But I did, and others have, too. In this chapter our voices recall this period of the grief journey. These voices—our voices— tell you that you, too, can come through this. Hear us as we tell you our stories of how our beloved pets continue to live on within us and touch our lives. Hold onto a notion of faith that if we could get through and beyond this, you can, too.

Some people in the midst of their excruciating pain may find these words unbearably hard to read. They may be offended by the suggestion of holding a notion of hope. They may feel disconnected to words that bear no resemblance to their experience. They may think no one else felt about their pet the way they did. There simply may be no way to relate to the idea of ever resolving *this* loss at *this* insufferably painful time. It may feel impossible to imagine that anything good or transformative could come from an animal companion's death.

". . . a time to heal . . . a time for peace . . ." reflects the experience of keeping one's connection to one's animal and holding on to memories while moving on to an evolved relationship. "A time to heal" conveys a sense of hope for healing and the possibility of transforming tragedy and sorrow into something positive. It also implies that one give oneself time for healing to occur. Time and grace do help in the healing process.

Memories can heal. ". . . Blessed are they that mourn, for they will be comforted. . . ."

KEEPING THE SPIRITUAL CONNECTION

People tell me evocative stories of their ongoing spiritual connections with their animal companions. I no longer hesitate to ask, "Do you still feel your animal's spirit?" Their voices reflect their conviction that their pets are part of them forever as they live on in spirit. A woman recently said she was comforted by a friend's statement: "The body gives up the struggle, but the soul and spiritual connection remain." For many, there are times when their animals still feel close. It's comforting to know that some part of their animal is still conscious and active. Whatever realm they're in, they're growing, learning, and deepening their awareness.

The following compelling stories show the powerful ongoing spiritual connection between a person and animal after death. Erica told of her experience with Mao:

Mao's spirit's all around me. Last September I had been reading what I'd written about his last twenty-four hours, and I was crying. I actually felt his spirit come into the room. It felt like he was big, like he took up the whole room. I didn't see him, but I felt this being coming up to me; and I thought, this feels like Mao. We had this conversation:

"Why are you crying?"

"Well, because you're gone."

"I'm right here with you. I'm all around you. I'm with you always."

"I know, but you're not physically here. I can't see you. I can't hold you."

"Is that really it? You have Patrick [her other cat]. You do have a cat you can be with, that you can touch."

"I can't hold Patrick; he doesn't like to be held, but I can have physical contact with him."

Mao was making me think about what was really going on.

"Well you know," I said, " you're right, it isn't really that."

Then I thought, what is this really about? Why am I really crying?

"It's just that I never wanted you to suffer and die the way you did."

And he said, "I know, my love, but it's all over now. I'm not suffering anymore. It's not part of my reality and existence anymore. If you want to come and cry on my shoulder for a while, you can, but you don't have to weep anymore. Let all your favorite autumn things comfort you. I'm all around you, I'm out in all the autumn things that you love so much."

So according to Mao, he's all around me. That's his word.

Erica still sets aside time every day to tell Mao how much joy he brought her and how glad she is that he came to live with her. She told me of the time she felt two hands reaching toward each other, one reaching up from her heart and the other reaching down to connect. This experience felt, to her, like a blessing, another manifestation of their continuing bond—Mao's way of saying, "Thanks, Mom."

Consider Scott's story. Jackie, his beloved black Lab, died on Valentine's Day, a day we recognize those we love. Several weeks later in Florence, Italy, on business, Scott came across a beautiful old church, in the corner of which were votive prayer candles. Scott asked God to take care of Jackie, letting her know how much he loved and missed her, and how sad he was that he wasn't able to be with her when she died. Scott wanted Jackie to know that when his time came, he'd be with her again. He finished his prayer by lighting one of the unlit candles from one already burning.

Twenty minutes or so later he went into a coffee shop to get out of the cold. As he laid his hands on the counter he saw, to him, something miraculous. Just below the base of his thumb on his right hand that had held the candle, was a disk of wax with a wavy edge. In the center of the disk was a transparent heart, made of wet wax, while the surrounding wax had solidified. Scott described the heart as perfectly symmetrical and flawless. He first thought how incredible it was that wax would dry that way. He suddenly realized he'd never even felt what probably amounted to fifteen drops of hot wax fall onto his hand. Furthermore, after walking outside in the cold air for over twenty minutes, the heart had remained liquid while every other part had hardened. Scott said:

I know it to be much more than an unexplained coincidence. To me it was a message from a loved one, a message which fit so perfectly with the symbolism of the day that I lost her and so well with the message that I asked God to give her. Jackie's sign meant, "I love you, too, and I am okay."

From that day on, a great part of the grief of Scott's loss was lifted, "All thanks to one final gift from a very special friend who had already given me nothing but happiness every day of her life for more than fourteen years."

Debra's relationship with Addison evolved as the months passed:

It's changing as the year's going on. In the first month or two, even though friends would tell me he was still with me, I'd try to feel him, but I didn't feel anything. After a couple of months I was thinking about him and thought, "I bet he does come down and keep an eye on me and make sure that Chloe [her new dog] is doing what she needs to do. I think he comes to make sure I'm doing what I told him I would do, which is go on and have a good life. And then, when he sees everything's okay, he goes back up to wherever he is and plays.

Debra learned from Addison that love that deep doesn't disappear just because he'd been cremated. She was able to move his ashes to a higher shelf, not needing them in front of her any longer. Also, she didn't need to carry his collar and tags, "Because he's in my heart now, I can put those other things away."

Patricia was reassured when she realized Auggie's spirit continued with her:

Something happened once that I didn't understand. I was sitting here, really sad. All of a sudden, these vertical blinds moved. That's what Auggie used to do, he'd walk up and down, his little trick. I just really had to wonder. The heater wasn't on. It wasn't like something hit the blinds. I think it was him coming back. I asked the psychic, "Is his spirit still alive and with me?" She said his answer was, "Yes, I've been back, and you know when those times have been. I'm always in your heart. I don't want to see you sad. I know you miss me, but know I'm always with you. I will continue to visit you until I know you're okay to carry on." It was very reassuring.

Things were different for Patricia after that. She could be sad because she physically missed him, but she could also have her conversations with him.

Tending My Fire—Remembering You

Early this morning I came in to build today's fire. The room was cold and dark. When I looked at the fireplace, it looked like the fire was totally gone. I saw only a pile of cold and gray ashes. There was total silence. But as I got the ash pan and shovel to remove the ashes, under the pile of ashes was a bed of embers, still burning and hot. The heat and light from last night's fire, the embers, still glowed today. Just as you do in my heart and memory. Last night's embers are the beginning of today's fire. All I had to do was blow on them and they flamed up to catch today's paper and wood to begin this morning's fire. Your ongoing presence and love in my life are the beginning of my life today. Just as there is a circle of life in the phases of a fire, there's a circle of life in your presence in my life. Just as the life of a fire seems short, so did your life. Just as a fire gives off heat and light, so did your life. Just as a fire gives out and dies, so did your life. And just as a fire still has those many burning embers, so does your life. This morning I remember you again as I enjoy today's fire. And I thank you as I gently place another log on and feel its warmth.

—Betty J. Carmack

For the past twenty-three years, Elinor has had overlapping cats. Because in her experience cats learn from each other, it's important for her to keep that chain going. All her cats have known each other or known of each other through the other cats. Now she feels that each cat who ever lived with her is still with her in some form or other because of her unbroken chain of cats. Every once in a while she feels like a specific former cat is still present because of a particular behavior of a current cat.

For some, their animals' visits in dreams bring comfort. Elinor's dream world is a place she continues to see and feel Idgie as well as other pets who have died. She wants to hold on to all her pets' memories, "They may not be important in the schema of the planet, but they're important in my life." Moving on doesn't mean forgetting.

Not everyone experiences this continued spiritual connection. Some are disappointed, surprised, or angry that they don't, especially when they'd shared such a close relationship. They're envious of others' stories of a continued spiritual link. They look for it, wait for it, and wish for it. Such was Sharron's experience:

> People say they can, but I just can't. I wish I was one of those people who can say that. I close my eyes and go there, but no, I don't feel her. All I feel is emptiness and loss.

For those who feel an ongoing spiritual connection, it is a powerful source of solace.

RITUALS/MEMORIALS

For those who choose to have an observance, a lot of thought, time, and love goes into the decisions. People want their final tributes to reflect their respect and love for their animal companions and symbolize their shared relationship. Honoring our beloved animal companions through rituals and memorials is a way of healing our grief. Rituals have the ability to focus, center, and calm us and convert something painful into something less painful. Participating in a memorial can be a transformative step, a factor in helping one move on while not forgetting.

On the other hand, some individuals are not able to carry out a memorial or ritual. Their emotions feel too out of control to consider a ritual. They fear their emotion would overwhelm them.

Rituals can be solemn and reverent, festive and celebratory, or both. Numerous individualized and creative ways of honoring animals have been used. Tender and poignant tributes are placed on Internet Web sites. Monetary donations are made to animal organizations. Memorial plaques, photo montages and still life tableaus are created. Candles are lit; plants, flowers, and trees are planted. Poetry and music are written as tributes. Scrapbooks, collages, memory books, diaries, art books, and journals have been created to honor a pet's place in a person's life. Letters are written to pets, some of which are put into the grave or placed with the body at the time of cremation. Other letters are kept in a safe and special place. Some have their pets' images painted onto plates. Ilana had Cris Kitty's life-sized portrait painted on a rock. Robert and Bonnie created a three-by-three foot collage of Basko on their wall. Additionally, they took one of their photographs of Basko and their son and had it scanned onto a pillowcase as a gift for him. Patricia created her "Auggie Garden," which she continually tends and into which she incorporates seasonal mementos. Pali had Leadbelly's face tattooed on her arm. She also created evocative art books as memorials to her dogs. She said thinking of her dog Esmo while using her hands to construct something allowed her to let the "horrible painful thoughts out." Janet keeps her dog Missy's bear friend, Fanny, right where Missy always sat. This past Christmas Janet was given a statue of Missy. "Now we have a permanent reminder of her right on the floor," she said.

Sally ensured that the presence of her cat, Nicholas, would continue in her life by creating his "Nicholas Tree." Ever since Nicholas died seven years ago, Sally has wanted to create a memorial to honor him. This past Christmas she bought a potted dwarf spruce tree, which she placed at the front of her home. She named the tree "Nicholas." She and her children decorated his tree with multiple bright decorations and lights. She lights the bulbs on the tree for family events such as graduations, birthdays, anniversaries, or weddings. In this way Nicholas continues to have an ongoing presence in Sally's family. She added that creating her "Nicholas Tree" in his honor was comforting.

The importance of creating a sacred space is fundamental to many rituals and memorials. Some people have chosen to create an altar or shrine in their home as a place of reverence. On it they may put the animal's ashes, photographs, flowers, a candle, and other mementos that have special meaning, such as the pet's collar, a special piece of nature, or a statue. Others include pieces of the pet's fur, whiskers, or hair. One woman had cut the long strands of hair from her dog's tail. She took strands of her own hair and intertwined these with his, tying them all together with a piece of mauve silk ribbon. Others save treasured mementos in special little boxes—whiskers, teeth, fluffs of fur, tags, and collars. To honor and remember her cats, Elinor has saved whiskers from all her cats during the past twenty years. Occasionally she takes some of the whiskers and places them into little piles of fur she's also kept. A few choose to have their pets freeze-dried.

Some include announcements of their animal's death with accompanying photographs on the obituary page of newspapers. Others send memorial cards, some with photographs, to announce a death. Patricia sent a photo of her and Auggie on a card on which she had printed:

Auggie Dog, August 18, 1985–August 1, 1998
Unconditional Love—Inconsolable Loss . . .

Some people choose burial for their animals. The sites vary— a pet cemetery, one's own property, the property of someone else. For these individuals it's important to be able to go to the site where the animal was placed into the ground. One couple buried their cat under a terrace beneath a fig tree in their garden, where they put a sculpture of a sleeping cat. Some place a statue of St. Francis near the grave.

Many incorporate rituals and memorials into the burial. Solemnity, spirituality, and reverence underlie many of these rituals. Some choose to bathe their animal before the burial. Others apply aromatic essential oils as part of the burial ritual.

Gates told me of the reverential burial of Blackie, her cat. She and her husband, Bill, prayed the Lord's Prayer and recited the twenty-third Psalm. Into Blackie's casket, Gates put his favorite toys and pictures of his human family as well as Ann Scott, their other cat who had predeceased him. Not only did Gates wrap him in sheepskin, she also lined his casket with sheepskin. Using bricks, she made crosses at each cat's gravesite. She also placed a statuary cat at the site where Blackie stood when he'd beg to come inside. Now when she sees this statue, she's reminded of her dear Blackie.

Ilana described the burial of her cats as both powerful and traumatic:

> It felt like we were burying our children. The visual image and memories of their burial is an experience that's never left me. It was helpful in that we had some closure and felt they were finally at peace, but it was hard to do, the actual burying, putting earth on them, and watching them disappear into that hole. We'd felt we were in limbo until we buried them. Afterward, it felt good to have done it.

A month later when she went back to visit the grave, a stray cat appeared, wandering around the garden and rubbing lovingly against her feet. He began eating the catnip Ilana had planted at the time of burial. Acting like neither Ian nor Cris Kitty, he was more like a combination of them. Ilana felt his watchful presence over them as if he knew they were buried there.

Ilana still feels she wants to go back and have a ritual. In her spiritual beliefs, at cemeteries one leaves a little stone on the grave as a symbol that one was there. She indicated that she would most likely go back, making sure the grave is alright.

Visits to pet cemeteries show the mindfulness, love, and care that goes into burying a beloved animal. Walking among the headstones and reading the inscriptions is a touching witness to the depth and power of love that's shared between persons and animal companions.

For Jyl there was definite comfort in the idea of burial: "While she was on the physical plane, I was her earthly mother, and now I've returned her to the bosom of Mother Earth. I think that's where she should be." Jyl buried Muffy in an open casket with a lace coverlet, over which she placed a beautiful delicate piece of rice paper with gold and silver flecks. Inside the casket she placed, in addition to Muffy's toys, a small pomegranate because of its symbolism of rebirth and new life. She also put a candle in to light Muffy's way. On handmade paper with pressed flowers Jyl wrote, "To Muffy, with all my love, Mommy." She told Muffy what a gift and blessing she'd been to Jyl's life, how she'd graced Jyl's life and would always live in her heart. Muffy was wrapped in Jyl's flannel pajamas because Jyl wanted something gentle caressing Muffy in her death, "since Muffy always caressed my life." She incorporated flowers into the burial service, which she described as, "So sad, horrendously painful, yet very healing."

Observing her Jewish tradition, the following year she planned to unveil a headstone that would incorporate Muffy's photograph with an inscription that said, "Muffy Bambi Cohen, October 1987 to June 1998, Goddess of Grace. Darling Muffy, Jyl's beloved soulmate. Your gentle presence graced my life for ten sweet years. You live forever within my heart."

Paule and Gina recalled the rituals they created for Sophia, their eighteen-year-old Brittany spaniel, and Pasta, their nineteen-year-old cat. Sophia died in June, Pasta a few months later.

For each animal Paule and Gina made a muslin shroud on which they sketched images of each pet doing its favorite things. Additionally, they wrote all the affectionate names they'd given Sophia and Pasta. After death, each animal was wrapped in its shroud, which was then tied with ribbons that were intertwined with flowers and sprigs of sage.

The veterinarian came to their home for each euthanasia. Those who had gathered for Sophia's passing sang lullabies to her. A wake was held with approximately twenty people present, including a Methodist minister. Earlier that day someone had dug Sophia's grave. Friends, serving as pallbearers, carried Sophia's body from the car and gently placed her in the grave, placing flowers on top of her. A neighbor, who loved Sophia as his own, brought music, and everyone sang to Sophia. The neighbor's wife brought a rose. In the Cherokee tradition, Gina performed a heart chant. Buddhist Prayers for the Dead were said. Some eulogized Sophia. The service ended with everyone singing, "When the Saints Go Marching In." The ritual for Pasta was similar.

Gina and Paule had already carefully selected beautiful pink alabaster rocks as headstones for both graves. Every year Paule honors both Sophia and Pasta on their birthdays when she goes to their graves and plants a wildflower for Sophia and catnip for Pasta.

Other persons prefer cremation for various reasons—some spiritual, some religious, some practical. Some choose an individual cremation so they get only their animal's ashes back. Others select group cremations, having animals cremated with others. Many elect to hold on to the ashes, wanting them close. Some individuals select containers that have particular meaning for them and place the ashes within. Often people keep the box of ashes close to their bed or put it under their pillow. Josie and Michael, who keep their dog Rosie's little wooden box of ashes by their bed, say they talk to her all the time and kiss the box every day. Janet keeps Missy's ashes in a cedar box atop a chest with photos of her and some of her favorite toys and gifts from her best friend, Sarah Elizabeth. One family buried some of their dog's ashes in the foundation of the new home they were building. Others sleep with the box as the pet used to sleep with them.

Robert and Bonnie decided to hold on to Basko's ashes for the time being. They knew they wouldn't be in their same house for the rest of their lives and wanted to be able to take his ashes when they moved. Some people plan to co-mingle the ashes with their own ashes or have them placed in their own casket at the time of their death. The longing to have one's pet share eternity is powerful for some pet parents.

Others scatter the ashes at special places. Typically, the ritual of scattering the ashes is very meaningful. Erica recounted her experience of scattering Mao's ashes:

I didn't want to let go. That was my last actual physical link with him. Part of me was saying, "But let go. He needs to be free; you need to be free. It's important, just let go." But another part of me didn't want to let go because it would be so final. I took the ashes to the ocean, found a cliff, and scattered them. Now they're rolling around with the tides. They'll turn into limestone some day.

I waited for a big gust of wind. Just at that moment, I took the container and closed my eyes and tossed the ashes into the wind, and I felt a feeling of release, glee, and celebration. It's like the wind had been waiting to carry his ashes, and finally it happened. It's like, we're doing okay now, let's go.

The wind didn't get all of them, though. Some stuck to the hillside. I kept going back every couple of weeks, because I felt like I had to guard them. Finally, when the winter rains washed them all down, I felt like it's okay now. There's nothing left for me to protect. It was kind of funny because there were a lot of pigeons flying around pecking grit, and I thought, "What if they eat one of the ashes. Usually it's the cat eats the bird, but now it's the bird eats the cat."

The comforting presence of another dog was important to Elaine as she scattered the ashes of Pumpkin, her golden retriever:

My husband and I took her ashes to our favorite vacation rental cabin where dogs are welcomed. The owners' dog, Hannah, came bounding down the hill as we passed her house. On all our previous visits, she had greeted us but then returned to her front porch. Today was different. Today Hannah stayed with us as we scattered Pumpkin's ashes along the paths and in the meadows filled with irises and buttercups. Hannah continued to stay with us, even accompanying us back to our cabin. As I played a recording of *Brahm's Requiem,* Hannah lay by my side. At its conclusion, Hannah nuzzled my hand and trotted back over the hill to her house. What did she know? What was she trying to communicate to us? There is no question that I was comforted by her presence. Additionally, she planted a seed that allowed us to adopt another dog eight months later.

Years ago I was invited to a celebration and memorial service for a beloved dog. The gentleman held the service in his back yard on a Sunday afternoon. On the fence, in a place of prominence, was a large painting of his dog. We sang songs in praise of God's animals, and he eulogized his dog. The service was followed by a celebratory feast.

I also shared a pizza meal honoring another beloved dog. Because pizza was one of his favorite foods, we feasted on his preferred style and type of pizzas. His pet mom wanted both to honor him and have support as she scattered his ashes. After eating our pizza and reminiscing about him, we scattered his ashes at some of his favorite neighborhood spots, such as near the fast food restaurant where his favorite burgers and fries were purchased.

I'm already thinking ahead to Sarah. I have a song planned to sing for her at the time of her passing. Several years ago, I heard the song "You Are My Beloved" from Jack Pantaleo's musical, *The Gospel According to the Angel Julius,* in which God sings to the angel, Julius:

. . . You are my beloved, and I'm so proud of you, when you come home, I'll hold you in my arms . . .

Both at that time and now, I believe in the appropriateness of the words for someone's passing. It's not only the words, it's the melody and the reverence with which they're sung.

I've also written a prayer for her:

For Sarah: Mother Earth, I place her in your arms now where I know you will hold her. I know your love will forever surround and protect her, just as her love will forever surround and protect me.

BRINGING A NEW ANIMAL COMPANION INTO ONE'S LIFE

People often struggle with knowing when it's time to bring a new animal into their lives. Some question if they can ever love another animal. Others feel betrayal and disloyalty to an animal who has died if they bring another animal into their home. Still others feel resentment toward a new animal now in the space and place that once belonged to their deceased pet. Those who think they'll never have another who can measure up to the one they've lost consider getting a different species altogether. Others say they'll never get another pet because it would be too painful to re-experience this same level of grief. Some fear the responsibility of another pet. They feel on some level they failed their deceased animal because they couldn't save it. Their fear that they might fail another animal prevents them from getting one. Patricia said:

I've had a couple of people ask me about getting another pet, but I just don't know. It used to make me nauseous thinking about it. In the beginning it would be like talking to some-body who'd just lost her husband and asking, "Are you going to date?" It made me feel like vomiting, it was so distasteful. I know there are a lot of dogs that need good homes, and I'm a good dog mom, but the thought of it was appalling.

When I see someone walking their dog, I want to say, "Do you know how lucky you are?" I want that so much in my life. I want to be part of that picture, and I think that's what makes me sad now. I'm not up for the challenge yet. I look at them and think, "You're so lucky, you just don't know."

On the other hand, some feel the finest tribute they can give to their deceased animal companion is to get another. "He'd want me to do that because he wouldn't want me to be alone." And, "With the number of animals that need a good home, she'd be mad if I just sat around and cried."

Some pet parents talk with their animal before its death, saying that when they get another, it will not mean they're trying to replace that animal. Instead, they simply have the love to give another. They ask for their animal's understanding and blessing of their plan to adopt. A man and his wife told me recently that they finally decided to bring a new animal into their lives eleven months later "when the guilt no longer drove us, and we could act more from a place of love than guilt." Others get another animal to help them endure their loss.

When I talked with Jody and Rachel, they were still reluctant about getting a new dog. They each acknowledged their ambivalence. Neither was ready to reinvest in another dog, wanting a longer time lapse between having Kasha, their thirteen-year-old Airedale who died two months earlier, and "another dog that we're going to fall in love with." Yet, each acknowledged missing "having a doggie friend" and doing the kind of things one does with one's doggie friend. Jody also recognized their sense of freedom in being able to travel as they pleased without the responsibility of arranging care for a dog.

Rob, too, was hesitant to bring a new dog into his life, although he acknowledged the "wonderfulness of the day-to-day companionship they provide." He expressed hope that he'd eventually get the courage to open himself up to a new dog, but he knew he wasn't ready yet.

It took Debra seven weeks before she was ready to open her home and heart to getting her new dog, Chloe. She acknowledged loving Chloe and developing a wonderful relationship with her. But at the same time, she felt her life with Chloe wasn't the same as her life with Addison—the routine they'd had all those years, his personality, his stubbornness, the differences in their behaviors. With Chloe, life was different. Chloe was more independent and didn't need to be as close to Debra as Addison did. It was a dissimilar relationship.

Some people don't search for a new animal companion or make a conscious choice to adopt. Instead, another pet finds them. Perhaps a new cat comes to their home. Or someone needs a home for a dog because a child has developed allergies or someone's parent is moving into a nursing home.

When I lost Rocky, I was looking for another dog by the third or fourth day. I simply could not stand the house being so lonely and quiet. It was unbearable not having an animal to care for, love, and hold. I went to the San Francisco Society for the Prevention of Cruelty to Animals and looked. The first day I came home alone.

Sometime soon after, perhaps the third time I went, I saw a little black puppy at the front of her cage, whining and pleading to be taken out. She had been brought in that morning, and she hated the cage. She was looking for someone to rescue her, and I was looking for someone to rescue me. I asked to hold her. I still remember her crawling up my chest and nesting her little head under my chin, leaning into my body. I adopted her. We needed each other.

I took her home on the bus. Why I didn't drive, I'm not sure. I still remember how surreal the experience was—the feeling of utter disbelief and unreality as I rode home holding her and trying to comprehend that she was my new dog.

I clearly remember the feelings of disorientation when I saw a little black furry terrier-like puppy where before there had been an adult reddish brown smooth-haired dachshund. Emotionally, it didn't feel real. Yet, I was trying to make it real because I knew intellectually that it was real.

I named her Puccini. During the next few weeks I did "puppy" things, like trying to housebreak her. She was cute and sweet and brought a new much needed energy to my home. But I remember not really loving her at that point. There wasn't the heart connection yet. I was grieving deeply for Rocky, still hoping he'd come home— still holding out that hope, which lessened as more time passed.

In a short period of time I did come to love Puccini, and she became a major presence and force in my life. We shared a lot of our lives together, and at the time of her death, only six years later, I deeply grieved her death and mourned her passing.

During the years I've come to realize that, for me, that lack of immediate heart connection has occurred each time I've brought a new dog into my life. Now I accept it and realize that, with time, feelings of love do develop. Others, too, have described that lack of immediate heart connection when they've brought a new animal into their home. There's a period of comparing the new animal to the previous one, a time of detachment while feelings settle down. For most people, in time, those feelings evolve into another heart connection. Patience and not judging oneself can help, as can the acknowledgement that, for many, these feelings are quite common and natural.

Sharron purposefully did not bring another animal into her life after Gigi's death. She was trying to wait a year because she didn't think adoption was the right step for her at that time. She described this year without a pet as "withdrawal." She hadn't been without something or someone to care for, and even though she'd liked to have had an animal, she felt strongly that she needed to spend time taking care of herself.

Steve had no intention of getting another bird. He knew if he did, it wouldn't be Porkchop. It wouldn't be that relationship; it would be a new one. He felt if he got a new bird now, he'd be distancing himself from her memory, which he didn't want to do. He didn't want her to feel as if he could replace her.

Robert and Bonnie didn't want to get a new dog too soon because they didn't want to be disrespectful. They also didn't want to bring new dogs into their home until they knew what their living situation would be. They were certain, though, that eventually they wanted puppies from the same bloodline as Basko. Robert knew that he'd tell them about their Uncle Basko.

Jyl found the experience of having a new cat to be a major adjustment that was upsetting and unsatisfactory. It was jarring to see a cat that looked so physically different. Every time she looked at Angel, her new cat, she thought, "You're not Muffy." Jyl felt it wasn't fair to Angel because she's trying to do something impossible, which is to replace an irreplaceable animal.

Others had pressured Jyl to get a new cat. They didn't want her to be sad and wanted her to do something to feel better. With hindsight, she knows she got a new cat to accommodate others' timelines, not her own. In retrospect, she realizes it would have been better if she'd waited.

LESSONS LEARNED

"How do you make sense of all this?" "What are the lessons for you?" "How are you different because of your animal's life and death?" I ask these questions regularly. It can be worthwhile and meaningful to reflect on the lessons learned from living with animal companions and what they've brought to our lives. For some it takes time for the answers to evolve. For others the lessons are readily apparent. An answer I hear often is that our animal companions teach us about unconditional love, patience, and caring. Because of our relationship with them, we are changed forever. When we made that covenant with them long ago, we pledged to keep our commitment to our animal companions. By keeping that commitment, they've become forever a part of our heart and memory, and we never lose that connection.

An overriding lesson is the transient nature of life and how suddenly people and animals can be gone. There's a new realization and appreciation of the sacredness of life, of everyone and everything. We have been reminded of what's important in life—family and unconditional love. There's a new appreciation of the preciousness of the time we have with our animals. "They're my children, my family, and I need to appreciate the time I have with them." People have said they want to spend more quality time with their animals, giving them love and attention.

One of Erica's lessons was about letting go of control:

I still see that I was powerless, but now I feel differently about it. I just accept that. Suddenly, everything fell into place. Everything happened exactly the way it was meant to happen for Mao's destiny. I now understand what my role was in this whole thing. I wasn't meant to be able to cure him with my love. I was meant to be there to assist him, but not to have any power or control over his destiny. That was an important lesson for me, that one little bit of illusion that I needed to remove from my consciousness. There's a limit to how much control we have.

Sharron described her lesson as learning to let go because so much of life is about losing what one has. "I just seem to have trouble getting that lesson." Because Sharron had lost her mother, sister, former boyfriend, partner, employee, and now dog, she questioned what she could possibly have that she wouldn't lose. Yet, she recognizes that if she hadn't lost her sister, she wouldn't have had Gigi. If her former boyfriend hadn't died, she wouldn't have been with Stan. Sharron's fundamental knowledge that good things can come from bad is what sustained her through her grief:

You get to the point where you think, "What is this all about?" It may be the process of life, but it's painful. We need to learn how to put the lessons of life and the choices we make with our lives into a spiritual context.

Jyl thought her spiritual lesson was that she needed to expand her world, reality, and lifestyle to a point where she could reach out to others, rather than stay in the safe, trusting, comfortable, familiar bubble she enjoyed with Muffy. She felt Muffy might be teaching her to embrace a connection with, enjoyment of, and comfort from nature.

Idgie's death was a catalyst for Elinor to be more caring for herself. She was reminded that in order to help others, she needs to care for herself first, "It's not an endless supply." Another lesson she learned was to be less accommodating and pleasing to others, unless she chooses to do so. Additionally, she learned she doesn't need to destroy herself and die with her animals. Idgie's death helped her recognize the importance of these lessons.

Because Debra welcomed friends and family bringing up Addison's name and remembering him, she learned that when she wants to mention a deceased loved one to a person, she should do so. "They'll tell me if they don't want to talk about it."

POSSIBILITY OF TRANSFORMATION

People speak and write about losses, deaths, and tragedies as grounds for change and transformation. Erica remembers reading about the menorah that Rabbi Harold Kushner says is his most meaningful because it's made from discarded pieces of junk metal. The story of that menorah symbolizes our ability to transform what looks like junk into something sacred, to make choices that are life affirming when all around us feels chaotic.

Erica's experience with Mao's death allowed her to transform her grief into a lesson of courage and compassion, "I felt more whole as a person having gone through such a tragedy."

Everyone's experience is different. I know that. Not everyone has a life-altering or transformative experience. Regrettably, some people don't heal, and their woundedness continues or worsens. For others the loss is real but doesn't lend itself to anything life-changing.

But others, with time and introspection, *can* look at their grief experience as life-changing. Through it, they've learned, grown, and become more whole. When I lost Rocky, I couldn't imagine that his death would be transformed into something positive. But in time it did.

I remember the day that I began to turn his death into something positive. I had gone into a beautiful old San Francisco Catholic church, one I had never gone into before. I don't even remember why I went into it that day. Perhaps it was providential.

When I got to the altar, I saw an image of Christ on a cross and reflected on his death. I thought to myself that I hoped I live my life always mindful of his gift for us in his death.

Thoughts are interesting—how we get from one to another without quite understanding the connective process. It wasn't long before I began thinking of how Rocky had died. I couldn't save us both, and he was the one to die. I absolutely could not let his death be in vain. That would be the second tragedy in his death—if I wasted my life and didn't make something positive out of it. I walked out of the church that day with a deeper appreciation of what Rocky gave so I could live. I had a new heightened awareness that he had died, and I was still alive.

Within the next three years, I had started my pet loss counseling practice, seeing clients individually as well as in pet loss support groups. Had it not been for Rocky's death and the way he died, I don't believe I would have thought of providing such a service. Because I had walked my own painful journey of grief, I was able to accept an inner call to begin such a service for others.

Now I can say, with conviction, that Rocky's death was not in vain. I was able to transform his tragic death into something positive, not only for myself, but for the lives of many individuals. Back in 1978, on that July day, I would never have believed such a transformation was possible.

Reconciling a loss and death usually takes time. A recurring theme is one of contemplation. With hindsight, people often get what they describe as a window into their souls. Erica experienced this:

I learned a lot about myself. I had no idea I had that kind of integrity or strength. When I was taking care of Mao, every day was crisis mode. When I was in the middle of that whirling energy, I wasn't really analyzing anything or myself. I was just, "Okay, can we make it through the next hour? Can we get through the next day?" It was only after it was all over that I asked, "Did I really do all that? Was that really me that did that?" I didn't know I had it in me. There's a saying that adversity builds character, but I don't think that's true. I think adversity reveals character. This whole experience was the universe's way of giving me a window deep into my soul, to see what I'm really made of. I truly did not know I had that much inner strength to deal with something so fragile and vulnerable.

One woman was able to look at her pet's death as a gift to her new stage persona in her performances. Elinor wanted to use her writing skills to do something educational related to the care of animals. Additionally, she wanted to focus her future volunteer work on activities related to animals and nature. She also acknowledged that she'd been taking extremely good care of herself since Idgie's death. She was more conscious of her personal health and felt his death would contribute to the furtherance of her own life and health. Robert and Bonnie used Basko's death as an opportunity to share with others the potential dangers of heat and altitude. They wanted others to be aware of what had happened so it need not happen to another dog. Steve said that telling Porkchop's story was a good way to honor her and her importance in his life. Telling her story was a way of reconciling his love for her with his decision to euthanize her. Perhaps it was that very love that gave him the strength to agree to let her go.

Patricia continues to reflect on the meaning and lessons of her experience:

I don't know the purpose yet. It may take some time to be seen. Part of it could be teaching me not to be surprised at how deep grief can be over something that you actually thought you had prepared for. Sometimes you don't realize the depth of your love for someone until you have to grieve their loss. Having gone through this with my pet, the most devastating thing in my life up until now, maybe I'll realize a little sooner that there wasn't anything more I had to say or do. I did everything I could.

RECONSTRUCTION OF ONE'S WORLD

After the death of her little dog, Rose Kennedy, Josie wrote, "Grief is a process. It feels like it has taken over your mind and body, the grip never leaving you, but that is not true. You do recover, albeit slowly."

Two years after her cat's death, Mileva's eyes filled with tears as she spoke of Abigail, "My eyes well, but my heart is full. I've had two years of a feeling of richness, not of sadness."

Patricia acknowledged some of her process of putting her world back together:

I listened to other people, and I tried to believe them because they looked like average normal people. They'd say, "Well, I got through it, it's very painful," this, that, and the other thing. Somehow I just didn't think I would be one of those people. I really thought I would not do as well as I have.

I believe there are different steps to healing. One's not "over" the grief at any particular time or in any particular way. For some it's been well over a year, or three years, or twelve years, or more—and they still don't feel they've resolved their loss. I'm not surprised. For many, the death of their animal companion rekindles other major issues for them. Some put the death aside as much as they can. Others actively work to resolve their issues. I've come to understand that grief is a process that some people don't necessarily ever "get over." Their grief may become more muted and less raw, but nevertheless it may still be there.

Rob echoed this sentiment as he struggled to reconstruct his world without Zomax:

> I don't feel at peace yet. I don't know how to get myself there, other than hoping that some time will help. I don't think the death of a loved one is something you're ever going to get used to. Maybe that's just part of it, too. To know that this is how it is, and that there isn't something you have to try to fix. Maybe you just live with it, and it is what it is. Maybe it doesn't need figuring out.

Someone recently told me that when she first heard people speak of still grieving for pets who had died two years previously, she thought, "How can I live like this for two more years? I loved my animal more than I loved my own life." Now three years after her cat's death, she returned to the support group.

In some ways, she says, it seems as if it was only yesterday that her cat died, but it also seems like a lifetime. Her cat's presence and spirit blessed her life for their years together. To have that taken away was devastating. She now feels her pain will always be present but will gradually become layered over, like a scar.

Others have said, and I agree, that it's important to trust one's own pacing and let one's own rhythms guide one through grief. People process experiences in different ways and in different time frames. Some need more time to grieve. Additionally, the particular circumstances of an animal's death can dramatically affect the grief process.

For many, reconstructing their world means holding onto the belief that they'll be reunited with their beloved animal companion. Looking forward to being together again is a hope that gives meaning to life. Sally, believing that heaven is a place where she will be reunited with her family and friends, hopes her little dogs will be there to greet her. She believes that if heaven is that beautiful, perfect afterlife, then Pudgy, Snoopy, Nicky, Boots, and Paddy Mac will be wagging their tails and licking her face. Patricia, as well, says she believes that pets go to heaven because it wouldn't be heaven without them. She now has a guardian angel, Auggie, who's watching over her. "I'm looking forward to being reunited with my precious Auggie in heaven."

Nancy, too, anticipates experiencing again the love of companion animals after her death: "I can't help but believe that if God is love, he wouldn't abandon any of his loving creatures, and pets are certainly that. Hopefully, he has a special place for them in heaven, and one day I'll experience this unconditional love again."

Holding on to the belief that a beloved animal companion does continue to dwell in one's heart can help those who are grieving. A person, grieving the loss of his cat in addition to other losses of family and friends, shared a quote he was given, "To live in the hearts of those we leave behind is to never die." There's a powerful sense of reassurance in this belief of a continuing presence in one's life.

That covenant we made so very long ago still endures. A love that strong doesn't end because an animal companion is no longer physically present. To make and hold a covenant—a pledge, a promise—implies continuance.

Additionally, the idea that these animals can and do protect and guide us is comforting. I once heard Oprah Winfrey say, "When you lose a loved one, you gain an angel whose name you know."

Taking this idea further, Janet personalizes this notion of animals' continuing guarding presence. She told her granddaughters, who both spoke about Missy and looked for her, that Missy is in the sky behind the moon, in heaven, watching and protecting them, "When you're afraid, look up. Missy will be there for you."

Now I leave you with the gift of holding onto a hope that healing can come—because others have gone through and beyond their unbearable grief. You've read the stories of our grief for our beloved animal companions. We've shared with you how we've come through the darkness of our grief into the light of healing. Our voices tell you that our relationships with our dearly loved animal companions do continue. They've left us a precious and valuable legacy. What we loved in their life, we continue to love.

It is true we mourned, but it is also true we found comfort. Hear and trust the enduring wisdom of the scripture passage, ". . . Blessed are they that mourn for they will be comforted . . ."

. . . a time to heal . . . a time for peace . . .